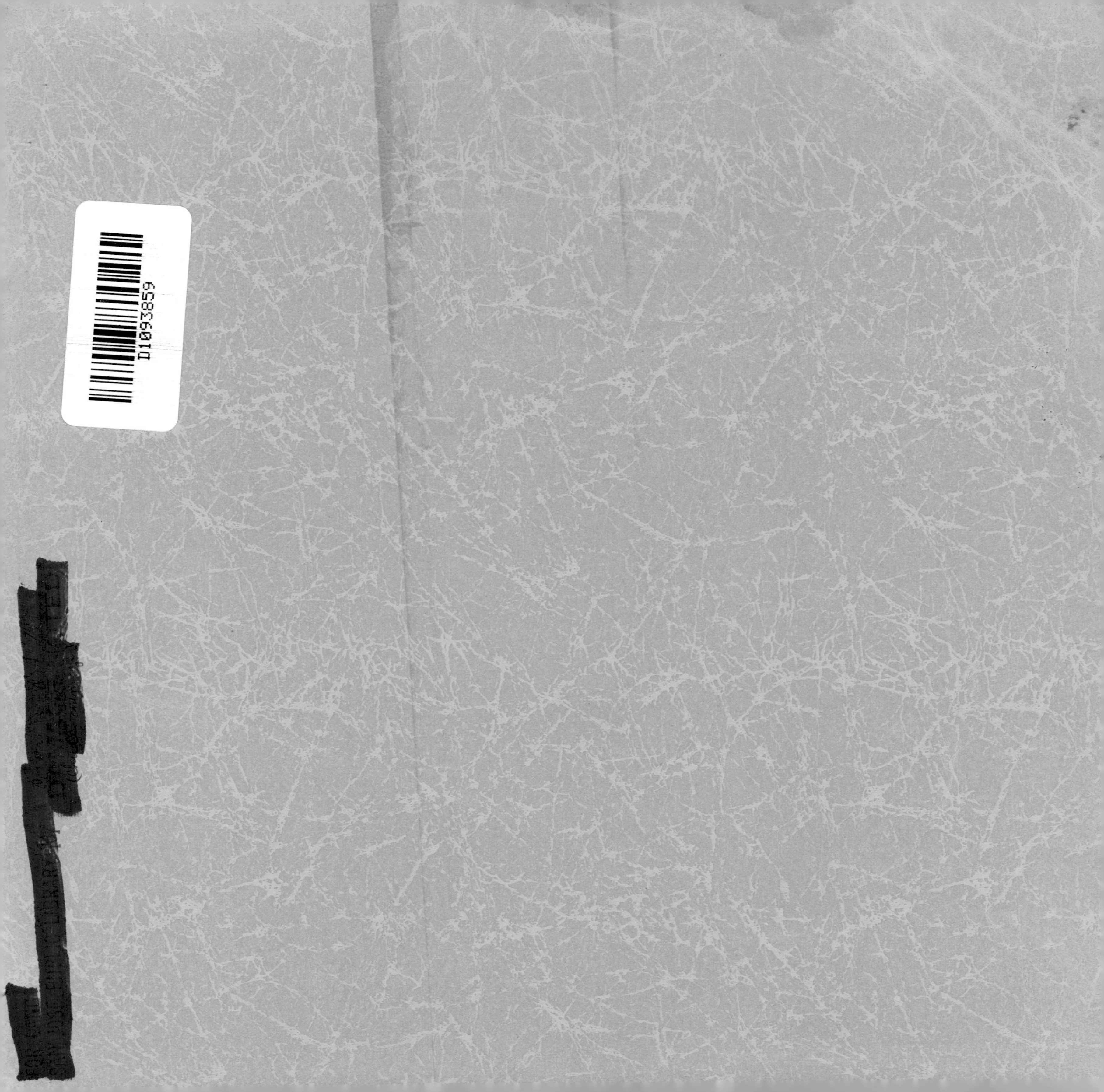

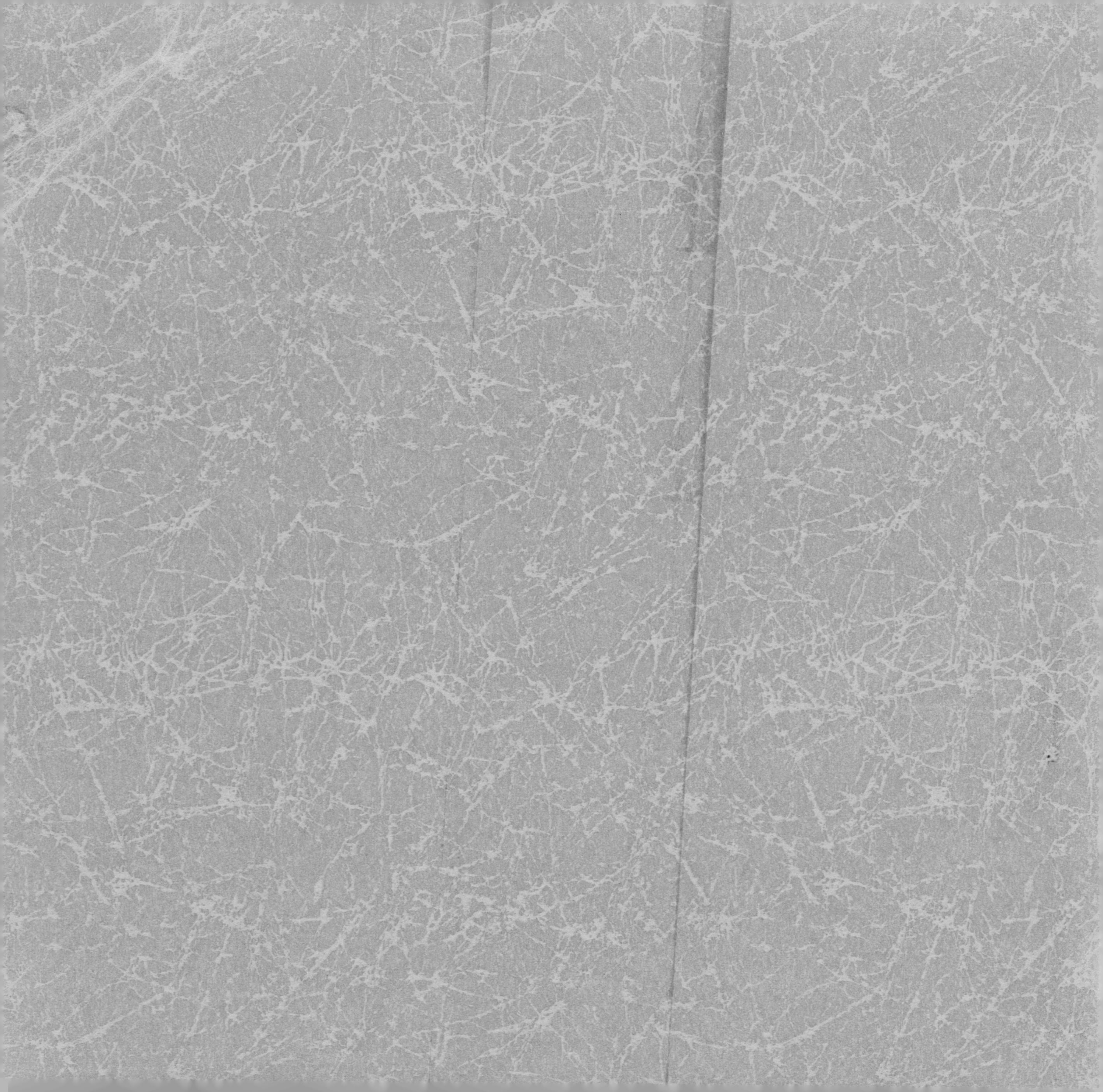

Japanese Garden

四季日本の庭

大橋治三 写真集

Each photo caption is described as follows :

Katsura Rikyu	*Stepping Stones*	*Momoyama Era*	*Kyoto*
Title	Item	Time	Located

Japanese Garden

1-9-12 Kudankita, Chiyoda-ku, Tokyo 102, Japan
ISBN4-7661-0366-1

Printed in Japan

First Printing, 1986

四季日本の庭

大橋治三
写真集

目 次　Contents

「四季日本の庭」寸感

草野心平（詩人）

私はいま退院後の静養のため，阿武隈山脈のなかの川内村という過疎村にある天山文庫に起居しているが，同じ部屋で同じ庭を見ながら，この一文を書く同じ机で「庭は永久に未完成」という詩を書いたことがある。その感懐は今も変らない。詩型などは除外して言葉だけを並べると，

　大小の岩や石だけの庭ならまだしも　水のない庭ならまだしも　樹木や羊歯のある庭は　永久に未完成である　木は育つ　木は枯れもする　苔も育つ　天の具合で水も変る　庭は瘠せる　天のドラマは庭にヂカだ　ドラマは愛撫し　また残虐に庭を崩す　一応夢が造型されても　植物は動物・眼には見えないが動いている　造型された輪郭は崩れる　これ庭の命運である　だからこそ自分は　庭甲斐に生きる　生きたい

というのだが，この感懐はいまも変らない。

茅ぶきの文庫の建物の設計は山本勝巳君だが庭の設計は私がやった。庭を初めてから今年で恰度二十年になる。ここは山の中腹にあるが，庭に関する限りゼニは一文もかかっていない。植木屋から買った木は一本もなく，クレーンで運んだ大石もただ，トラックも莫大な労働力も全部ただだった。

村内にある山なら，公私に拘らず，そこの樹木や石たちも，いくら運んでも文句は言はれなかった。ブルトーザアで山腹をけずりとった庭は，初めは，それこそ一木一草もなかった。どんな庭にしたらよいか見当もつかなかったが，思案の末，樅と栗の大きな枯木を掘り起こし，その三本を植えたことから庭作りを初め，そして「庭は永久に未完成」という詩を書いたのである。

ところでこの「四季日本の庭」に掲載される大橋治三さんの写真は全部で九十六枚，そのうち京都の庭は四十六枚，他は青森から鹿児島，そして沖縄まで，日本列島を縦に貫いている。

私は大橋さんが何年・何十年に亘って庭園への愛を内心燃やし続けたかを知らない。またどのようなプランのもとに撮影をはじめられたかをも私は知らない。けれども私は知ることが出来る。氏の異常とも言へる庭園への執心と，これらを撮り終えたエネルギーとを。（曽てタウトやハーンがいた。けれども欧米その他の人々のどれだけが，日本の庭園を知ってるだろうか。これらの蒐集は日本的美を彼等に納得してもらふ一つのチャンスにならないだろうか。）

ところで私は拙詩のなかで，砂利だけの庭ならまだしも，と書いているが，その時私は龍安寺の石庭を對照の一部に考えていた。草木とちがって石は不動だからである。けれども一夜の豪雨によって，あの砂利に描かれている美しい線は消えるだろう。「まだしも」も絶対ではない。忽然襲はれた「未完」である。「未完」でないためには庭園はまた原型にもどらなければならないだろう。

西芳寺の苔の庭はあれでいい。けれどもあの苔群のなかに雑草が生えればマイナスである。私は雑草を軽侮してはならない。雑草は庭のために必須の場合がある。その可否は人間と雑草の会話によって決められる。苔をきらう石，苔好きの石も，或る必然によって帰趨が決められる。樹木は植物であると同時に動物であるから，常に動揺する。私は健康な時でも年に一回はここで起居するが，その度ごとに庭の表情は変貌する。私にとって庭は永久に未完成だが，堂々の原型は不変であるべきものであろう。それは庭を創る夫々の人の夢であり，夢は造園の原型をもたらす言はばポエジー如きものであるだろうと思われる。

大橋さんに誘発されて私は脱線しかかっている。いや最初から私は脱線した。それもこれらの写真による誘惑であり，その誘惑が私にとっては爽かだった。そして（曽てタウトやハーンがいた……）を最后にもう一度繰返したい。と真実私は思う。

JAPANESE GARDEN (A BRIEF IMPRESSION)

SIMPEI KUSANO (Poet)

I am presently living at Tenzan Bunko in a depopulated village called Kawauchi located in the mountain range of Abukuma recuperating following my discharge from the hospital. I sat and wrote this poem, "A Garden is Never Finished", at this same desk I have sat in day after day in the same room gazing at the same garden. Even now I feel the same emotions stirring in me. This is the poem.

A garden of only large rocks and small stones may be fine.
A garden of merely pebbles alone may be fine.
A garden of no water flowing may be fine.
However, with trees, shrubs, and ferns
A garden is never finished.

A tree grows, withers and dies.
A shrub grows, withers and dies.
And moss grows.
As water changes with the whims of heaven,
The garden becomes famished.

The drama of the heavens pervades.
It may caress or lay rage.
The plant ivy like a living creature
Moves unseen by all except by nature.
Its contours is demolished.

This is the fate of the garden.
My life dies and relives with the fate of the garden.
Wishing to live such a way.

This feeling will stay forever with me.

At Tenzan Bunko, Katsumi Yamamoto designed the thatched roof bunko (library), while I designed the garden. It has been 20 years since I first started on the garden. Located at the breast of the mountain I did not use a single yen in its construction. Not a tree or shrub was brought from the nursey. The gigantic rocks brought in by cranes and trucks in addition to the tremendous amount of labor were all free of cost. Within the range of the mountains in my village no public or private expenses were entailed and no matter how many trees or rocks I had them transport not a grievance was voiced. In the beginning the garden, which was craved out in the middle of the mountain by bulldozer, did not have a single tree or blade of grass. Lacking plans on what kind of garden I wanted, I dug up some large withered maple and chestnut trees after some consideration and planted the three trees. This initiated the construction of my garden. I, then, wrote the poem, "A Garden is Never Finished".

Overall, Haruzo Ohashi's pictures comprise of 96 photographs in this book, "Japanese Garden." Among them, 46 were taken of Kyoto gardens and the others ranged from Aomori to Kagoshima and Okinawa running vertically through the Japanese archipelago.

I had no idea of Ohashi's secret love for gardens over these numerous years of acquaintance. I don't know what plans he had when he first set out to photograph gardens however I do know that there is no other like him with such a strong devotion to gardens investing the energy to portray them.

(There were Tauto and Hurn, however, I wonder how much westerners know of Japanese gardens. This collection is one chance to acquaint others with the beauty of Japan.)

In my poem when I wrote the line that "A garden of merely pebbles alone may be fine", I had intended to partially contrast it with the rock garden at the Ryoan-ji Temple. Differing from trees and plants, rocks are immobile, although the beautiful lines and ripples can be demolished by one night of heavy rain. The term, "may be fine", is not absolute. It becomes "unfinished" by the unexpected ravage. To prevent it from being "unfinished" the garden must be repaired back to its original form.

The moss garden at the Saiho-ji Temple is nice, however, if there are weeds growing among the moss, it is marred. I do not scorn weeds. As a matter of fact, there are some instances where they are necessary for the garden. Its propriety is decided by the dialogue between man and weed. Also whether moss adheres to rocks, it is determined by natural consequences. Garden plants are plants, but at the same time they are living creatures as evidenced by their trembling. When I was healthy I always came up here once a year and each time the garden's features underwent a transformation. To me a garden is forever unfinished. Perhaps its grand original form should be constant. Growing a garden is everyone's dream and this dream produces the original form of the garden. I believe it is as stated in the poesy.

Induced by Ohashi, I became derailed. No, I was derailed in the beginning, but above all, I was enticed by the pictures. The enticement was refreshing. I truly want to repeat here again that (there were Tauto and Hurn.....)

Calligraphy: Kuniko Ishihara

題字：石原都子

Design: Hiroto Kumagai

デザイン：熊谷博人

Editorial Director: Kakuzo Akahira

エディトリアル・ディレクター：赤平覚三

1 桂離宮 飛石 桃山時代 京都
Katsura Rikyu Stepping Stones Momoyama Era Kyoto

2 桂離宮 書院前庭 桃山時代 京都
Katsura Rikyu The Front Garden of the Study Room Momoyama Era Kyoto

3 京都御所 御涼所前中島 江戸時代 京都
Kyoto Imperial Palace Osuzumi-sho Maenakajima Edo Era Kyoto

4 修学院離宮 上の茶屋 江戸時代 京都
Shugaku-in Rikyu Kami no Chaya Edo Era Kyoto

5 修学院離宮 西浜暮色 江戸時代 京都
Shugaku-in Rikyu Nishihama at Sunset Edo Era Kyoto

6 修学院離宮 上の茶屋雪景 江戸時代 京都
Shugaku-in Rikyu The Snowy Kami no Chaya Edo Era Kyoto

7 大仙院 枯滝石組 室町時代 京都
Daisen-in Karetaki Stone Grouping Muromachi Era Kyoto

8 大徳寺 枯滝石組 江戸時代 京都
Daitoku-ji Karetaki Stone Grouping Edo Era Kyoto

9 相国寺 枯山水 江戸時代 京都
Sokoku-ji Karesansui Edo Era Kyoto

10 両足院 枯山水 江戸時代 京都
Ryozoku-in Karesansui Edo Era Kyoto

11 銀閣寺 銀沙灘 室町時代 京都
Ginkaku-ji Ginsanada Muromachi Era Kyoto

18–19

12 竜安寺 枯山水 室町時代 京都
Ryoan-ji Karesansui Muromachi Era Kyoto

13 西芳寺 苔の庭 鎌倉時代 京都
Saiho-ji Moss Garden Kamakura Era Kyoto

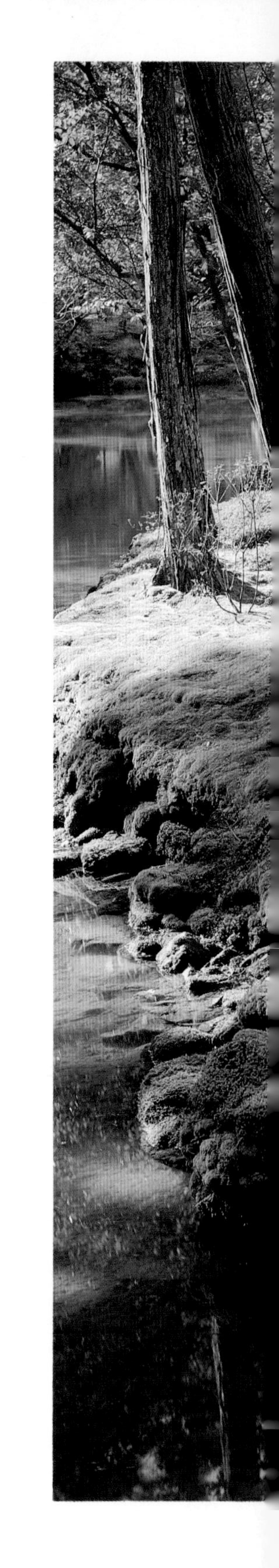

14 西芳寺 中島付近 鎌倉時代 京都
Saiho-ji Around the Island Kamakura Era Kyoto

15 仙洞御所 池庭中央部 江戸時代 京都
Sento Imperial Palace The Central Part of Chitei Edo Era Kyoto

16 天竜寺 滝石組 鎌倉時代 京都
Tenryu-ji Taki Stone Grouping Kamakura Era Kyoto

17 浄瑠璃寺 全景 平安時代 京都
Joruri-ji A Complete View Heian Era Kyoto

18 金閣寺 全景 鎌倉時代 京都
Kinkaku-ji A Complete View Kamakura Era Kyoto

19 金閣寺 滝石組 鎌倉時代 京都
Kinkaku-ji Taki Stone Grouping Kamakura Era Kyoto

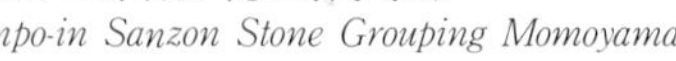

20 三宝院 三尊石組 桃山時代 京都
Sanpo-in Sanzon Stone Grouping Momoyama Era Kyoto

21 二条城 護岸石組 桃山時代 京都
Nijo-jo Gogan Stone Grouping Momoyama Era Kyoto

22 智積院 滝石組 江戸時代 京都
Chijaku-in Taki Stone Grouping Edo Era Kyoto

23 桂離宮 岬燈籠 桃山時代 京都
Katsura Rikyu Misaki-gata Lantern Momoyama Era Kyoto

24 真如院 瓜実燈籠 桃山時代 京都
Shinnyo-in Urizane-gata Lantern Momoyama Era Kyoto

25 成就院 全景 江戸時代 京都
Joju-in A Complete View Edo Era Kyoto

26 本法寺 枯滝石組 桃山時代 京都
Honpo-ji Karetaki Stone Grouping Momoyama Era Kyoto

27 真如院 全景 桃山時代 京都
Shinnyo-in A Complete View Momoyama Era Kyoto

32–33

28 曼殊院 石橋石組 江戸時代 京都
Manshu-in Ishibashi Stone Grouping Edo Era Kyoto

29 西本願寺 亀石組 江戸時代 京都
Nishi Hongan-ji Kame Stone Grouping Edo Era Kyoto

30 金地院 鶴石組 江戸時代 京都
Konchi-in Tsuru Stone Grouping Edo Era Kyoto

31 一休寺 東庭枯山水 江戸時代 京都
Ikkyu-ji Karesansui at the East Garden Edo Era Kyoto

32 霊雲院 全景 室町時代 京都
Reiun-in A Complete View Muromachi Era Kyoto

33 南禅寺 全景 江戸時代 京都
Nanzen-ji A Complete View Edo Era Kyoto

34 東海庵 中庭全景 江戸時代 京都
Tokai-an A Complete View of the Courtyard Edo Era Kyoto

35 表千家 残月亭付近 桃山時代 京都
Omote Senke Around the Zangetsu-tei Momoyama Era Kyoto

36 裏千家 又隠付近 江戸時代 京都
Ura Senke At the Yuin Edo Era Kyoto

37 武者小路千家 中門付近 江戸時代 京都
Mushanokoji Senke At the Middle Gate Edo Era Kyoto

38 藪内宗家 待合付近 江戸時代 京都
Yabunouchi Soke Around the Machiai Edo Era Kyoto

39 孤蓬庵 山雲床蹲踞 江戸時代 京都
Koho-an Sanunjo Tsukubai Edo Era Kyoto

40 表千家 不審庵蹲踞 桃山時代 京都
Omote Senke Fushin-an Tsukubai Momoyama Era Kyoto

41 武者小路千家 官休庵蹲踞 江戸時代 京都
Mushanokoji Senke Kankyu-an Tsukubai Edo Era Kyoto

42 聖衆来迎寺 書院前手水鉢 桃山時代 滋賀
Shojuraigo-ji A Water Basin Momoyama Era Shiga

43 東海庵 一文字手水鉢 江戸時代 京都
Tokai-an Ichimonji Water Basin Edo Era Kyoto

44 桂離宮 桂垣 桃山時代 京都
Katsura Rikyu Katsura-gaki Momoyama Era Kyoto

45 金閣寺 金閣寺垣 鎌倉時代 京都
Kinkaku-ji Kinkakuji-gaki Kamakura Era Kyoto

46 孤蓬庵 矢来垣 江戸時代 京都
Koho-an Yarai-gaki Edo Era Kyoto

47 藪内宗家 鉄砲垣 江戸時代 京都
Yabunouchi Soke Teppo-gaki Edo Era Kyoto

48 清藤氏盛美園 滝石組 明治時代 青森
Mr. Seido's Seibi-en Garden Taki Stone Grouping Meiji Era Aomori

49 毛越寺 中島石組 平安時代 岩手
Motsu-ji Nakajima Stone Grouping Heian Era Iwate

50 陽山寺 中央部大刈込 桃山時代 秋田
Yosan-ji Ookarikomi at the Central Part Momoyama Era Akita

51 玉川寺 全景 江戸時代 山形
Gyokusen-ji A Complete View Edo Era Yamagata

52 輪王寺 中央部出島 江戸時代 栃木
Rinno-ji The Central Island Edo Era Tochigi

53 能仁寺 滝石組 江戸時代 埼玉
Nonin-ji Taki Stone Grouping Edo Era Saitama

54 建長寺 全景 江戸時代 神奈川
Kencho-ji A Complete View Edo Era Kanagawa

55 旧芝離宮 池庭中央部 江戸時代 東京
Kyu Shiba Rikyu The Central Part of Chitei Edo Era Tokyo

56 長楽寺 池庭と築山 江戸時代 静岡
Choraku-ji Chitei and Tsukiyama Edo Era Shizuoka

57 満光寺 三尊石組 江戸時代 愛知
Manko-ji Sanzon Stone Grouping Edo Era Aichi

58 恵林寺 滝石組 鎌倉時代 山梨
Erin-ji Taki Stone Grouping Kamakura Era Yamanashi

59 大善寺 築山集団石組 江戸時代 山梨
Daizen-ji Tsukiyama Shudan Stone Grouping Edo Era Yamanashi

60 地蔵寺 全景 江戸時代 長野
Jizo-ji A Complete View Edo Era Nagano

61 永保寺 梵音厳の滝 鎌倉時代 岐阜
Eihou-ji Bonnongan Falls Kamakura Era Gifu

62 兼六園 琴柱燈籠 江戸時代 石川
Kenroku-en Kotoji-gata Lantern Edo Era Ishikawa

63 輪王寺 多層塔 江戸時代 栃木
Rinno-ji Multi-story Stone Tower Edo Era Tochigi

64 楽々園 大角燈籠 時代不詳 滋賀
Rakuraku-en Daikaku-gata Lantern Era Unspecified Shiga

65 後楽園 螢燈籠 江戸時代 岡山
Koraku-en Hotaru-gata Lantern Edo Era Okayama

66 兼六園 成巽閣露地 江戸時代 石川
Kenroku-en Seisonkaku Tea Garden Edo Era Ishikawa

67 清水園 滝石組 江戸時代 新潟
Seisui-en Taki Stone Grouping Edo Era Niigata

68 朝倉氏館跡 諏訪館跡石組 桃山時代 福井
The Site of Mr. Asakura's Residence Suwakan Ato Stone Grouping Momoyama Era Fukui

69 兼六園 池庭中島 江戸時代 石川
Kenroku-en The Island of Chitei Edo Era Ishikawa

70 西明寺 全景 江戸時代 滋賀
Saimyo-ji A Complete View Edo Era Shiga

71 大池寺 全景 江戸時代 滋賀
Daichi-ji A Complete View Edo Era Shiga

72 北畠神社 護岸石組 室町時代 三重
Kitabatake-jinja Gogan Stone Grouping Muromachi Era Mie

73 円満院 全景 江戸時代 滋賀
Enman-in A Complete View Edo Era Shiga

74 普門院 枯滝石組 江戸時代 和歌山
Fumon-in Karetaki Stone Grouping Edo Era Wakayama

75 根来寺 滝石組 江戸時代 和歌山
Negoro-ji Taki Stone Grouping Edo Era Wakayama

76 天徳院 枯滝石組 桃山時代 和歌山
Tentoku-in Karetaki Stone Grouping Momoyama Era Wakayama

77 法華寺 全景 江戸時代 奈良
Hokke-ji A Complete View Edo Era Nara

78 願行寺 全景 桃山時代 奈良
Gangyo-ji A Complete View Momoyama Era Nara

79 頼久寺 鶴島と大刈込 桃山時代 岡山
Raikyu-ji Tsurushima and Ookarikomi Momoyama Era Okayama

80 後楽園 池庭中央部 江戸時代 岡山
Koraku-en The Central Part of the Chitei Edo Era Okayama

81 深田氏庭園 石橋と三尊石組 鎌倉時代 鳥取
Mr. Fukada's Private Garden Stone Bridge and Sanzon Stone Grouping Kamakura Era Tottori

82 縮景園 中島と石橋 桃山時代 広島
Shukkei-en The Island and the Stone Bridge Momoyama Era Hiroshima

83 医光寺 亀島 室町時代 島根
Iko-ji Kameshima Muromachi Era Shimane

84 小川氏庭園 全景 室町時代 島根
Mr. Ogawa's Private Garden A Complete View Muromachi Era Shimane

85 桂氏庭園 全景 江戸時代 山口
Mr. Katsura's Private Garden A Complete View Edo Era Yamaguchi

86 栗林園 中島 江戸時代 香川
Ritsurin-en The Island Edo Era Kagawa

87 栗林園 全景 江戸時代 香川
Ritsurin-en A Complete View Edo Era Kagawa

88 兼六園 雁行石橋 江戸時代 石川
Kenroku-en Gangyo Stone Bridge Edo Era Ishikawa

89 後楽園 八ツ橋 江戸時代 岡山
Koraku-en Yatsuhashi Edo Era Okayama

90 多聞寺 滝石組 鎌倉時代 徳島
Tamon-ji Taki Stone Grouping Kamakura Era Tokushima

91 願勝寺 全景 鎌倉時代 徳島
Gansho-ji A Complete View Kamakura Era Tokushima

92 保国寺 全景 室町時代 愛媛
Hokoku-ji A Complete View Muromachi Era Ehime

93 千如寺 中島付近 江戸時代 福岡
Sennyo-ji Around the Island Edo Era Fukuoka

94 森氏庭園 滝石組 江戸時代 鹿児島
Mr. Mori's Private Garden Taki Stone Grouping Edo Era Kagoshima

95 水前寺 全景 江戸時代 熊本
Suizen-ji A Complete View Edo Era Kumamoto

96 石垣氏庭園 全景 江戸時代 沖縄
Mr. Ishigaki's Private Garden A Complete View Edo Era Okinawa

写真解説

Explanation of Photographs

1 **桂離宮**　飛石　桃山時代　京都
回遊式庭園の様式を持つ桂離宮はどこを切り取っても美の極致を見せる。変化に富んだ飛石が随所に見られ我々を誘導する。石と苔との肌合いは日本庭園の原点と言える。
SINAR P NIKKOR 210mm F5.6 f22 1/15 EPR

2 **桂離宮**　書院前庭　桃山時代　京都
桂離宮の顔ともいえる書院前庭。八条宮智仁親王と二代智忠親王が造営。二代の造営にもかかわらず計算しつくされた構成美は他に類を見ない完成度を持っている。
SINAR P NIKKOR 90mm F4.5 f22 1/15 EPR

3 **京都御所**　御涼所前中島　江戸時代　京都
池庭の広さ約二千百坪、池中に三つの島を置く御内庭御涼所付近は流れを強調した構成で飛石、石橋、護岸石組の変化に富んだ景観は四季折々の花々と共に、雅びの世界を現出する。
SINAR P FUJINON 210mm F5.6 f22 1/15 EPR

4 **修学院離宮**　上の茶屋　江戸時代　京都
修学院の美しさは雄大な自然と人工との調和がかもし出す美と言へる。桜咲く春、真紅に燃える秋、雪舞ふ冬、いつの季節でも訪れる者を裏切る事はない。
LINHOF KARDAN NIKKOR 90mm F4.5 f22 1/15 EPR

5 **修学院離宮**　西浜暮色　江戸時代　京都
これ程に自然を取り入れた庭園は他にはない。上の茶屋紅葉谷付近から見た西浜の夕景は、人工的な要素がありながら、それを感じさせないダイナミックさである。
LINHOF KARDAN NIKKOR 90mm F4.5 f16 1/2 EPR

6 **修学院離宮**　上の茶屋雪景　江戸時代　京都
雪の修学院はより一層自然美と人工美の極致を見せる。降りしきる雪中での撮影はつらかったが、改めて帝王後水尾院の、雄大な企画性と此の地を選び設計した発想の妙に感動した。
LINHOF KARDAN NIKKOR 90mm F4.5 f8 1/60 EPR

7 **大仙院**　枯滝石組　室町時代　京都
枯山水庭園を代表する作品。三十一坪の狭い空間に深山幽谷を表現する。深山からの流れが大河に変わり、やがて大海となる。白砂で象徴する流れの発想は日本庭園独自のもの。
LINHOF KARDAN SYMMAR 150mm F5.6 f22 1/4 EPR

8 **大徳寺**　枯滝石組　江戸時代　京都
巨石で何かを象徴する表現手法は種々あるが、此の三石による枯滝表現は、江戸初期によく見られる手法で豪華な力強い構成を見せる。中心に据えた石は水分石を表わす。
LINHOF KARDAN FUJINON 210mm F5.6 f22 1/4 EPR

9 **相国寺**　枯山水　江戸時代　京都
禅寺にふさわしく簡素な平庭枯山水庭園である。全体に明快、闊達な表現となっている。昭和に東部の岩組を一部改造した。後部に築山を配し平庭と築山の二重構造となっている。
SINAR P SUPERANGULON 75mm F8 f8 1/15 EPR

10 **両足院**　枯山水　江戸時代　京都
白砂での抽象表現は、流れ、大河、大海を象徴する外に、漣、渦巻き、市松等を表わす。この写真の渦巻砂紋は、狭い空間を広く見せると共に清潔感を強調している。
SINAR P SYMMAR 150mm F5.6 f22 1/15 EPR

11 **銀閣寺**　銀沙灘　室町時代　京都
足利義政は特に庭を愛した。彼の作庭による此の庭園を特徴づけるものに、銀沙灘がある。東側月待山から月が昇り始めると、この盛り砂が銀色に輝き、極楽浄土の世界が現出する。
SINAR P NIKKOR 90mm F5.6 f22 1/15 EPR

12 **竜安寺**　枯山水　室町時代　京都
白砂の中に十五個の石が点在する。大海中の島々を想ふのもよし、又虎の児渡しと見るのもよし。見る人の心によって変化する融通無碍の世界。哲学する庭と言えよう。
LINHOF KARDAN SUPERANGULON 75mm f22 1/8 EPR

13 **西芳寺**　苔の庭　鎌倉時代　京都
石と水と苔は庭を構成する大事な要素だ。特に西芳寺の苔は有名。手を触れるとほんわかした手触りは赤児の肌に似ている。梅雨頃の目に染みる青さが忘れ難い。
LINHOF KARDAN SYMMAR 150mm F5.6 f22 1/8 EPR

14 **西芳寺**　中島付近　鎌倉時代　京都
夢想国師が入寺する前から庭は作られていたが延元四年、西芳浄土寺に入寺、西芳寺と改めた。全山を覆う幽邃な雰囲気は俗世を離れ浄土への憧憬が増す。
SINAR P NIKKOR 90mm F4.5 f32 1/2 EPR

15 **仙洞御所**　池庭中央部　江戸時代　京都
修学院と共に後水尾院ゆかりの大池庭。造営は、永緑十二年に始まり小堀遠州がその指揮をとる。南池には栗石敷の州浜があり、その曲線は特に美しく四季の花々がそれに色を添える。
SINAR P NIKKOR 90mm F4.5 f22 1/15 EPR

16 **天竜寺**　滝石組　鎌倉時代　京都
この奥部滝石組附近は、蘭溪道隆の作品、石橋、滝石組、鯉魚石、遠山石、どれ一つ取ってもその造形力はすばらしく、豪快な力強さを示し、石組技術は日本庭園中の白眉。
SINAR P FUJINON 210mm F5.6 f22 1/2 EPR

17 **浄瑠璃寺**　全景　平安時代　京都
別名九体寺という。池の西側に阿弥陀堂があり九体の仏像を安置する。最近池庭全体を整備し面目を一新した。池面に映ゆる阿弥陀堂の姿に平安の面影を残し、見る人を引きつける。
SINAR P NIKKOR 90mm F4.5 f22 1/4 EPR

18 **金閣寺**　全景　鎌倉時代　京都
足利義満の建立。昭和二十五年焼失、同三十年に再建された。広い池庭に大小十に余る島があり、金色の影を落す水面に昔の栄華が偲ばれる。
LINHOF KARDAN NIKKOR 90mm F4.5 f22 1/15 EPR

19 **金閣寺** 滝石組 鎌倉時代 京都
天竜寺滝石組と共にその構成は秀逸。中央部水落ちの所に天に昇る竜を表現した鯉魚石が見える。今にも動き出しそうな、そんな感じのする石組である。
LINHOF KARDAN SYMMAR 150mm F5.6 f22 1/2 EPR

20 **三宝院** 三尊石組 桃山時代 京都
三尊仏の姿から来ている三尊石組、阿弥陀を中心に観音、勢至その他釈迦三尊、薬師三尊等がある。この石組の中心石は藤戸石と言い秀吉が信長から受け継ぎ、ここ三宝院に入れた。
LINHOF KARDAN FUJINON 210mm F5.6 f22 1/8 EPR

21 **二条城** 護岸石組 桃山時代 京都
慶長六年、家康がこの地に築城した。池泉庭園の場合、必ずと言ってよい程、護岩石組が築庭上大事な要素となる。丹念に選ばれた石が優れた手法の下で息づき、光り輝やく。
LINHOF KARDAN FUJINON 210mm F5.6 f22 1/15 EPR

22 **智積院** 滝石組 江戸時代 京都
書院北端から見た滝石組だが、鎌倉時代の滝石組と比べると迫力がない。しかし緻密さ繊細さに於ては、この時代が優る。その形は定形的でなく自由闊達な表現である。
LINHOF KARDAN FUJINON 210mm F5.6 f22 1/15 EPR

23 **桂離宮** 岬燈籠 桃山時代 京都
石燈籠には色々な形があり、それぞれにネーミングされて各々、それなりの歴史を持っている。ここに見られる岬燈籠は多くの岬の中でも典型的なものである。
LINHOF KARDAN FUJINON 210mm F5.6 f22 1/15 EPR

24 **真如院** 瓜実燈籠 桃山時代 京都
真如院庭園（後述）内に置かれている燈籠。江戸中期頃の無縫塔（墓石）を利用して火袋をうがち燈籠としたもの、これには足利将軍義昭公の銘名によるという伝説があるのが面白い。
ZENZA BRONIKA ZENZANON 150mm F3.5 f16 1/30 EPR

25 **成就院** 全景 江戸時代 京都
隣りにある清水寺はよく知られた観光寺院。そのざわめきから遠のいてうその様な静寂さを保つ成就院の池庭は、清冽な水を湛へて美しい。ここには自然を借景とした優雅な造形が展開する。
LINHOF KARDAN SUPERANGULON 75mm F8 f22 1/15 EPR

26 **本法寺** 枯滝石組 桃山時代 京都
陶芸、蒔絵、書に精通した光悦の作庭として有名。特にこの枯滝の見所は、下部に据へられた縦縞模様のある石を水の流れに擬しているところだ。上部の枯滝部分と共にその創作性は素晴しい。
LINHOF KARDAN SYMMAR 150mm F5.6 f22 1/2 EPR

27 **真如院** 全景 桃山時代 京都
白砂で流れを表わし栗石敷で州浜を想わせる手法は、今迄に述べた。他にこの庭は鱗石を敷きつめて大河を抽象化している。ダイナミックで華麗だ。それはこの時代の作庭の特徴をよく捉えている。
LINHOF KARDAN NIKKOR 90mm F4.5 f22 1/8 EPR

28 **曼殊院** 石橋石組 江戸時代 京都
この庭を拝観して一番始めに目につくのがこの石橋である。中央奥部に橋添石を一段高く組み、その下を渓流が流れている。その構成は気宇広大で作者の力量が窺える。
LINHOF KARDAN FUJINON 210mm F5.6 f22 1/8 EPR

29 **西本願寺** 亀石組 江戸時代 京都
別名「虎溪の庭」と言われるこの二百三十坪の枯山水の中に枯滝、二つの石橋、力強い水分石、鶴亀石組、またこの頃流行の蘇鉄を植栽している。その景観は堂々としていて日本庭園中の傑作と言える。
LINHOF KARDAN FUJINON 210mm F5.6 f22 1/15 EPR

30 **金地院** 鶴石組 江戸時代 京都
前面にゆるいカーブを持って広がる白砂の向こう側真ん中に礼拝石を据へ、左に亀島、右に鶴島を作り鶴亀両島を主体とした庭は、明るく雄大である。特に鶴首石は堂々としている。
LINHOF KARDAN NIKKOR 90mm F4.5 f22 1/15 EPR

31 **一休寺** 東庭枯山水 江戸時代 京都
一休宗純は生前自分の墓をここに作り、文明十三年この地に示寂された。御廟前庭、南庭、北庭、東庭と四ヶ所に庭が設計されている。東庭は十六羅漢の庭と呼ばれて禅院らしいムードを持つ。
LINHOF KARDAN FUJINON 120mm F8 f22 1/8 EPR

32 **霊雲院** 全景 室町時代 京都
妙心寺塔中にある本院は個性の強い庭だ。十八坪の狭い庭に巨石を中心に放射状に組まれた石は何を意味するのか、力強く豪快でたっぷりした量感は凄い迫力を持つ。
LINHOF KARDAN NIKKOR 90mm F4.5 f32 1/2 EPR

33 **南禅寺** 全景 江戸時代 京都
南禅寺周辺は京都の中でも一際風光明媚な所、白砂に囲まれた石組は極端に土塀側に片寄せられている。この手法は大徳寺本坊の庭にも見られこの時代の特徴を捉えている。
SINAR P NIKKOR 90mm F4.5 f22 1/15 EPR

34 **東海庵** 中庭全景 江戸時代 京都
今回収録した庭の中で最も狭く小さい庭。全面積十二坪半の枯山水。一直線上の配石は変化に富み渡り廊下に仕切られた空間にぴりっとした緊迫感が漂う。文化十一年、東睦和尚の作庭。
SINAR P NIKKOR 90mm F4.5 f22 1/8 EPR

35 **表千家** 残月亭付近 桃山時代 京都
千利休の一子、少庵が利休の切腹のあと千家を再興する。露地には不審庵、残月亭、点雪堂等の席があり手入の行き届いた植栽は幽邃な雰囲気をかもし出し別世界へと誘う。
LINHOF KARDAN SUPERANGULON 75mm F8 f22 1/2 EPR

36 **裏千家** 叉隠付近 江戸時代 京都
千利休の孫元伯宗旦から裏千家は始まる。露地には今日庵、叉隠、寒雲亭、無色軒、咄々斎、抛筌斎、対流軒等の席がある。露地は侘の頂点として識者に高い評価を得ている。
LINHOF KARDAN SUPERANGULON 75mm F8 f22 1/2 EPR

37 武者小路千家　中門付近　江戸時代　京都
宗旦の第二子、一翁宗守が隠居する時現在の武者小路小川東の地に官休庵を建てる。写真は露地の中門付近であるが、ひなびた柿葺の網笠門で草庵の風情がにじみでていて、心安まる。
LINHOF KARDAN SUPERANGULON 75mm F8 f22 1/2 EPR

38 藪内宗家　待合付近　江戸時代　京都
初代剣仲紹智は織田信長に茶道役として任へていた。三千家と違って書院式茶道を中心として共に茶道会に大きく貢献している。この待合も貴人席と相伴席とを区別している。
LINHOF KARDAN SUPERANGULON 75mm F8 f22 1/4 EPR

39 孤蓬庵　山雲床蹲踞　江戸時代　京都
孤蓬庵忘筌の席は茶席の中でも最も有名なものであるが、写真に示す山雲床の席は、侘びた草庵風な露地で布泉の蹲踞と呼ぶ。茶の世界が広く普及することを願って小堀遠州が創案した。
LINHOF KARDAN FUJINON 120mm F8 f16 1/2 EPR

40 表千家　不審庵蹲踞　桃山時代　京都
表千家露地は侘草庵に徹し切った露地で深山幽谷の景を凝縮した様な別世界をつくっている。この蹲踞もこれにふさわしいムードを持ち、用の美と形式美とを兼ね備えている。
LINHOF KARDAN FUJINON 120mm F8 f22 1 EPR

41 武者小路千家　官休庵蹲踞　江戸時代　京都
石造の宝篋印塔や層塔の塔身を利用した蹲踞で四つの面に仏像を彫り出してある。四方仏の蹲踞と呼ばれ有名茶席、露地などで広く使用され名品が多い。
LINHOF KARDAN SYMMAR 150mm F5.6 f22 1/2 EPR

42 聖衆来迎寺　書院前手水鉢　桃山時代　滋賀
比叡山東麓に建てられた本院は恵心僧都の開基。鎌倉中期の宝塔の笠を裏返して柱杭の円柱に乗せ、手水鉢にしたもので別名、「日月の手水鉢」と呼ばれている。どっしりした重量感が美しい。
LINHOF KARDAN FUJINON 210mm F5.6 f22 1/4 EPR

43 東海庵　一文字手水鉢　江戸時代　京都
水穴を一文字風に彫り込んであるのでこの名がある。表千家や官休庵の蹲踞はしゃがんで口をすすぐが、これらの手水鉢は立ったまま口をすすぐ。縁先手水鉢とも呼ぶ。
LINHOF KARDAN FUJINON 210mm F5.6 f22 1/4 EPR

44 桂離宮　桂垣　桃山時代　京都
日本は竹の多い国で茶室や数寄屋造りに多く利用されている。ここに示す竹垣は桂離宮入口左側に廻らした囲いである。端正なデザインは心地良く、結界を示している。
LINHOF KARDAN SYMMAR 150mm F5.6 f22 1/8 EPR

45 金閣寺　金閣寺垣　鎌倉時代　京都
囲垣の一種で四つ目垣の変形である。普通の四つ目垣はこの写真の様に上部に冠せ竹を使用しない。四つの間隔が荒く背が低いその飾り気のない武骨な感覚が茶人によろこばれる。
LINHOF KARDAN FUJINON 120mm F8 f22 1/8 EPR

46 孤蓬庵　矢来垣　江戸時代　京都
孤蓬庵入口、石橋付近にしつらへてある竹垣で、豪放な構成美を持っている。はっきりした拒否の姿勢がうかがわれ、力強くたくましい竹の先が鎗のように尖っているのが特徴。
LINHOF KARDAN SYMMAR 150mm F5.6 f22 1/4 EPR

47 藪内宗家　鉄砲垣　江戸時代　京都
直径12cm余りの丸竹を縦に裂き、それを束ねて交互に重ね合わせ、棕櫚縄で結び、組み上げる、藪内宗家の露地にありまろやかな柔和な感じは矢来垣の持つ拒否感はない。
LINHOF KARDAN SYMMAR 150mm F5.6 f22 1/8 EPR

48 清藤氏盛美園　滝石組　明治時代　青森
江戸で活躍した大石武学が、この地に来て多くの庭を手がけ武学流庭園が大流行した。その弟子の一人小幡亭樹が作庭した。技法は的確な石組に江戸初期の手法が随所に見られ美しい。
LINHOF KARDAN FUJINON 210mm F5.6 f22 1/8 EPR

49 毛越寺　中島石組　平安時代　岩手
平安時代の庭は殆んど大池庭である。その池庭中に須弥山式石組があるのは当寺のみ、創建当時、宮殿楼閣三宇があり、二十一間もの反橋が架けられ浄土世界を現出していたという。
LINHOF KARDAN SYMMAR 150mm F5.6 f22 1/8 EPR

50 陽山寺　中央部大刈込　桃山時代　秋田
刈込みの庭というと頼久寺、大池寺、慈光院等があるが、当寺の刈込みのスケールは大きく大波小波を表現している。地割は異っているが頼久寺に似ている。東北には珍らしい刈込みの庭。
LINHOF KARDAN SYMMAR 150mm F5.6 f22 1/8 EPR

51 玉川寺　全景　江戸時代　山形
池泉観賞式で書院後庭に造られている。山畔に滝を落し池泉に三つの島を配する。背景の木立は深く自然と調和し細部の石組も鋭く強い。全体がダイナミックで美しい。
LINHOF KARDAN FUJINON 120mm F8 f22 1/8 EPR

52 輪王寺　中央部出島　江戸時代　栃木
男体山、輪王寺本堂を借景としスケールは大きい。東西にのびた池泉は九百五十七坪、つつじ、さつきの植栽が多く美しい。数少い関東庭園の中の名園と言えよう。
LINHOF KARDAN NIKKOR 90mm F4.5 f22 1/8 EPR

53 能仁寺　滝石組　江戸時代　埼玉
埼玉県唯一の名園。山畔を利用した池泉庭園で手入れが行き届いている。右手山畔部に組まれた滝石組は力強く豪華である。洞窟石組、石橋、護岸石組等当時の手法を残し今に伝えている。
LINHOF KARDAN FUJINON 210mm F5.6 f22 1/8 EPR

54 建長寺　全景　江戸時代　神奈川
建長五年、大覚禅師が当寺を開創した。山内には文化財、寺宝が多く観光客が絶へない。その喧噪の中、本庭の持つ清楚な地味なたたずまいは深い植栽と調和して、派手な石組こそないがつつましく美しい。
LINHOF KARDAN NIKKOR 90mm F4.5 f22 1/8 EPR

55 **旧芝離宮** 池庭中央部 江戸時代 東京
戦災で大破したが戦後東京都の手により復元され美しい姿を取り戻した。中島に中国風の橋が架けられ異国的なムードを醸し出している。中島山畔に江戸時代の石組が残されている。
LINHOF KARDAN NIKKOR 90mm F4.5 f22 1/8 EPR

56 **長楽寺** 池庭と築山 江戸時代 静岡
山畔築山には百本に及ぶ満天星が植えられ「満天星の庭」の別名がある。小堀遠州の作庭とされ当地方を代表する庭。自然を取り込んだ景観は、雄大である。
LINHOF KARDAN NIKKOR 90mm F4.5 f22 1/8 EPR

57 **満光寺** 三尊石組 江戸時代 愛知
本庭は庫裏の裏庭にありうっそうたる自然林に囲まれている。築山全体に石組があるという感じで滝石組、蓬萊石組、三尊石組ありで絢爛たる様は見る者を圧倒する。
LINHOF KARDAN FUJINON 210mm F5.6 f22 1/8 EPR

58 **恵林寺** 滝石組 鎌倉時代 山梨
「心頭滅却すれば火自ずから涼し」で有名な名刹である。一番古い個所は築山上部の須弥山石組、その外は家康と吉保等が修補し現在に至る。各部に洗練された手法が見られ巧みな庭と言える。
LINHOF KARDAN FUJINON 210mm F5.6 f22 1/8 EPR

59 **大善寺** 築山集団石組 江戸時代 山梨
本尊薬師如来は国宝であり「ぶどう薬師」の別名を持つ名刹。行基創建と伝へる。左隅築山には須弥山風、鶴島風の石組が共在し、その手法は豪快な力強さを示し一見に価する。
LINHOF KARDAN FUJINON 210mm F5.6 f32 1/4 EPR

60 **地蔵寺** 全景 江戸時代 長野
本堂裏の書院南東に、清冽な湧水を利用して作られた本庭は幽玄なムードに満ちている。奥深く入り組んだ地割に重厚な植栽が水面に映へ、その美しさは倍加する。
LINHOF KARDAN NIKKOR 90mm F4.5 f22 1/4 EPR

61 **永保寺** 梵音厳の滝 鎌倉時代 岐阜
鎌倉時代の名僧夢想国師の開創になる。開山堂は国宝、無際橋に仕切られた池庭の西側にこの梵音厳の滝がある。明るい庭内に流れ落ちる水音は清浄な感をたたへ、来観者を魅惑する。
LINHOF KARDAN SYMMAR 150mm F5.6 f22 1/8 EPR

62 **兼六園** 琴柱燈籠 江戸時代 石川
大名庭園として名高い兼六園は加賀百万石二代藩主前田利長公の時代に始まる。この広い庭内の名物はこの琴柱燈籠、遊覧コースの始めにあり記念写真を撮る人、ここに群がる。
LINHOF KARDAN SYMMAR 150mm F5.6 f22 1/8 EPR

63 **輪王寺** 多層塔 江戸時代 栃木
日光輪王寺庭園中島にある多層塔、本格的な多層塔は供養の為のものであるが、庭園に使用される場合、点景物、景を引き立てる為の要素が強く照明のものではない。
LINHOF KARDAN NIKKOR 500mm F8 f22 1/4 EPR

64 **楽々園** 大角燈籠 時代不詳 滋賀
燈籠には照明、献燈、供養、装飾等の使用目的がある。この燈籠は築山の上にあり左横に石橋、下に苑路がありその照明と景物を兼ねている。現代では景物としての要素が強い。
LINHOF KARDAN FUJINON 210mm F5.6 f22 1/8 EPR

65 **後楽園** 螢燈籠 江戸時代 岡山
平大鼓形の燈籠は珍らしい。火袋の上部に釣り燈籠を固定する鉤がありつり下げる様になっている。延養亭へ流れる川に沿ってしつらへられてあり昔日は盛んに使用されたであろう。
MAMIYA RZ SEKOR 180mm F4.5 f16 1/15 EPR

66 **兼六園** 成巽閣露地 江戸時代 石川
前田家百万石の十二世斉広公の夫人隆子の隠居所として作られた、曲水式の露地で珍らしい、雪の多い地方なので軒内に飛石が打たれていて独特な構成となっている。
LINHOF KARDAN FUJINON 120mm F8 f22 1/2 EPR

67 **清水園** 滝石組 江戸時代 新潟
池泉廻遊式の庭で東部池庭に桂離宮を意識した荒磯出島があり、突端に岬燈籠が置かれている。新発田藩主溝口家の下屋敷で植栽も美しく格調の高い風情を見せている。
LINHOF KARDAN SYMMAR 150mm F5.6 f22 1/4 EPR

68 **朝倉氏館跡** 諏訪館跡石組 桃山時代 福井
当庭園には写真に示す諏訪館跡、御湯殿跡、南陽寺跡の三ヶ所あり、共に桃山時代の豪快豪建な石組を残す。枯滝と蓬萊を兼ねた巨石の立石は見る人を圧倒する迫力を持っている。
LINHOF KARDAN FUJINON 210mm F5.6 f22 1/2 EPR

69 **兼六園** 池庭中島 江戸時代 石川
霞ヶ池と瓢池の上下二部の池庭から成っている。江戸始めから末期にかけて手が加えられ今日の姿となった。山崎山から流れ出る清冽な流れは、曲水曲流となって庭園内を駆けめぐる。
LINHOF KARDAN FUJINON 210mm F5.6 f22 1/2 EPR

70 **西明寺** 全景 江戸時代 滋賀
湖東三山の一つ西明寺の草創は古く平安時代に溯る。その本坊裏庭に位置する池庭は、再三の水害に遭い規模が小さくなったが、山畔に組まれた枯滝や蓬萊は当時の姿を伝えていて美しい。
LINHOF KARDAN NIKKOR 90mm F4.5 f22 1/4 EPR

71 **大池寺** 全景 江戸時代 滋賀
三重の大刈込みは大海波を表わし、手前左側の船形刈込みは、宝船の意味を持つ。滋賀県は石造美術の宝庫、庭園の宝庫とも言われる位庭の数が多い。当寺はその中でも異色の作品と言える。
LINHOF KARDAN SYMMAR 150mm F5.6 f22 1/8 EPR

72 **北畠神社** 護岸石組 室町時代 三重
もと北畠国司館の庭であったが後に神社となった。曲水式の池庭は護岸石組が随所に見られこの時代の質実剛健な気風が充満している。特に神木の下に組まれた枯山水は力強い。
LINHOF KARDAN FUJINON 120mm F8 f22 1/2 EPR

73 **円満院** 全景 江戸時代 滋賀
三井の晩鐘で有名な園城寺三井寺の塔頭子院の一つで円珍の創建という。宸殿の前庭に鶴亀二島があり、枯滝、護岸も優美で春は桜、秋は紅葉に調和し雅やかな趣がある。
LINHOF KARDAN SYMMAR 150mm F5.6 f22 1/8 EPR

74 **普門院** 枯滝石組 江戸時代 和歌山
弘法大師開基で有名な高野山には多くの寺院がある。本院もその一つで北に大きく亀島を作り石橋二つを架ける広がりのある庭で、多くの人が訪れる。夏は避暑で賑わい冬は雪で閉ざされる幽冥の地である。
LINHOF KARDAN FUJINON 210mm F5.6 f32 1/2 EPR

75 **根来寺** 滝石組 江戸時代 和歌山
書院北庭に設けられた庭で山畔に三段落ちの流滝を組み、その向こうに遠山石を置く。池庭には鶴亀二島、それに二つの石橋を架け洗練された手法を見せる。外に洞窟、夜泊石を作り景観は美しく見応えのある庭である。
LINHOF KARDAN FUJINON 210mm F5.6 f32 1/2 EPR

76 **天徳院** 枯滝石組 桃山時代 和歌山
高野山山内で最も古く由緒のはっきりした庭。加賀前田利常公夫人の菩提を弔う為、元和八年創建。庭は少し荒れているが写真に示す枯滝は三尊式で、雄渾な石組は力があってすばらしい。
LINHOF KARDAN FUJINON 210mm F5.6 f32 1/2 EPR

77 **法華寺** 全景 江戸時代 奈良
開基は光明皇后で尼寺である。本尊木造十一面観音像は光明皇后がモデルといわれる平安期の秀作。美しい池庭に土橋が架けられ、流れに小石を敷き優美な趣は尼寺に似つかわしい。
LINHOF KARDAN NIKKOR 90mm F4.5 f22 1/8 EPR

78 **願行寺** 全景 桃山時代 奈良
近くに桜の名所吉野山があり、シーズンには花見客で賑わう。枯池部分に栗石を敷きつめ築山には蓬莱石組を組む。石橋風に組まれた洞窟石組はこの庭の見所。狭い空間は明るく明快で引き締まった緊迫感を持つ。
LINHOF KARDAN NIKKOR 90mm F4.5 f22 1/8 EPR

79 **頼久寺** 鶴島と大刈込 桃山時代 岡山
小堀遠州が松山城主となった慶長九年頃この寺に作庭した。刈込みのみで大海波を表現する大胆な発想は滋賀の大池寺にもあるが当寺の方が古くその抽象的な構成はすばらしい。
LINHOF KARDAN SYMMAR 150mm F5.6 f22 1/8 EPR

80 **後楽園** 池庭中央部 江戸時代 岡山
庭園中央に唯心山と呼ぶ築山がある。その上からの眺めが一番良いが、写真に示した岡山城を望むアングルも捨て難い。所々に石組、曲水、燈籠、八ッ橋、四阿、延養亭等があり、見るべき物が数多くある。
LINHOF KARDAN NIKKOR 90mm F4.5 f22 1/15 EPR

81 **深田氏庭園** 石橋と三尊石組 鎌倉時代 鳥取
後醍醐帝が隠岐遷幸の折、当家を行在所にされたという由緒ある家柄。当時の庭園が数百年もの間、個人の手に依り保存された事は奇跡と言える。三尊石組、鶴亀石組等、見応えがあり当地方を代表する名園である。
LINHOF KARDAN NIKKOR 90mm F4.5 f22 1/2 EPR

82 **縮景園** 中島と石橋 桃山時代 広島
二十年八月の原爆で大破したが六年後に再建復元された。茶人の上田宗箇の造庭。築山、州浜、渓谷、滝等、廻遊式にふさわしい景趣を持ち、四季折々に変化する光景は美しくて楽しい。
LINHOF KARDAN FUJINON 210mm F5.6 f22 1/8 EPR

83 **医光寺** 亀島 室町時代 島根
画聖雪舟が益田氏に招かれ入山した折の作庭。中島となっている亀島は写実性を持ち理解しやすい形である。今にも動き出す様な流動感だ。山畔の枝垂桜咲く頃の庭は特に美しい。
LINHOF KARDAN SYMMAR 150mm F5.6 f22 1/8 EPR

84 **小川氏庭園** 全景 室町時代 島根
小川家は室町初期当地方に大きな勢力を持ち、和木将軍と称されていた。山畔に組まれた護岸、枯滝は選び抜かれた石材と共に強い構成力を示す。特に中央部枯滝は豪快極りなく、当庭園見所の一つ。
LINHOF KARDAN NIKKOR 90mm F4.5 f22 1/8 EPR

85 **桂氏庭園** 全景 江戸時代 山口
何とも言えない不思議な庭。全国に石庭数ある中で、特異な存在と言える。石を組むというよりも、石の上に石を乗せるという手法は他に類がなく、この石庭のみ。「月の桂」の別名を持つ。
LINHOF KARDAN NIKKOR 90mm F4.5 f22 1/8 EPR

86 **栗林園** 中島 江戸時代 香川
面積二十三万坪の公園に年間百五十万もの人々が訪れる。特に目につく赤松、黒松の樹林は見事なもので、手入れもさることながら二百三十年の伝統の重みが我々を引きつける。
LINHOF KARDAN FUJINON 210mm F5.6 f22 1/8 EPR

87 **栗林園** 全景 江戸時代 香川
飛来峰からの眺めがこの写真。スケールの大きな紫雲山を背景に偃(エン)月橋、西湖、掬月亭の景観は美しくすばらしい。大小六つの池と十三の築山を廻るには小半日はかかる広さ。天下の名園と言える。
LINHOF KARDAN FUJINON 120mm F8 f22 1/8 EPR

88 **兼六園** 雁行石橋 江戸時代 石川
園内を流れる清流は多量の湧水を利用している。この写真のあたりは曲水風になっていて流れも清く澄んでいる。亀甲形の板石を雁行に架けた石橋はこの庭独自なもので有名な作品となっている。
LINHOF KARDAN SYMMAR 150mm F5.6 f22 1/8 EPR

89 **後楽園** 八ッ橋 江戸時代 岡山
石橋、土橋、木橋等、材質の違い、架け方の違いは様々である。この八ッ橋は単に板を互い違いに並べ架けだという単純なもので、歩きながら目前の景色が変化するというアイデアはすばらしい。
LINHOF KARDAN SYMMAR 150mm F5.6 f22 1/8 EPR

90 **多聞寺** 滝石組 鎌倉時代 徳島
四国には名園が多い。中でも徳島には造形力の優れた庭が揃っている。古くから阿波青石の生産地であることが影響しているのかもしれない。堂々とした骨太な石組は小さな敷地から飛び出しそうに見える。
LINHOF KARDAN FUJINON 210mm F5.6 f22 1/4 EPR

91　**願勝寺**　全景　鎌倉時代　徳島
多聞寺同様小庭である。滝石組付近は、天竜寺竜門瀑にそっくりで、遠山石、鯉魚石も揃っていて豪華な作りが目を引く。往古、水が流れていたであろうが現在は枯滝となり下部の池も枯れている。
LINHOF KARDAN NIKKOR 90mm F4.5 f22 1/4 EPR

92　**保国寺**　全景　室町時代　愛媛
池泉観賞式庭園で地割は変化に富み、石組が各所にある。中央部枯滝は雄渾な手法で時代をよく表している。玄人好みの庭で意識的に植栽を避け石組がよく見える様に手入れされているのは好ましい。
LINHOF KARDAN FUJINON 120mm F8 f22 1/4 EPR

93　**千如寺**　中島付近　江戸時代　福岡
雷山千如寺大悲王院と言い、かつて一山三百坊あったという大寺。書院の前庭で幽邃な木立に囲まれ紅葉の頃は美しい。石組は荒廃しているが、二つの中島があり静寂な趣は心安まる。
LINHOF KARDAN NIKKOR 90mm F4.5 f22 1/2 EPR

94　**森氏庭園**　滝石組　江戸時代　鹿児島
森氏庭園のある知覧町は、元海軍特攻隊の基地。このあたりは武家屋敷が並んでいて、各家に枯山水庭園があり観光客で溢れている。その内、森氏庭のみは池泉式で石組は沖縄の庭に似ている。
LINHOF KARDAN FUJINON 210mm F5.6 f22 1/4 EPR

95　**水前寺**　全景　江戸時代　熊本
この地は湧水に恵まれている。透明な水面に富士形の築山が映え、訪れる人に強烈な印象を与える。寛永十四年細川忠利が築庭に着手した。南北に三島あり沢渡りでこれをつないでいる。
LINHOF KARDAN NIKKOR 90mm F4.5 f22 1/8 EPR

96　**石垣氏庭園**　全景　江戸時代　沖縄
沖縄本島は完全に戦災で破壊されたが、石垣島は辛くもまぬがれた。現存する本庭を本土の庭と関連して考える時、より参考になる。作者は首里の庭師間親雲上。築山の石組その他に海蝕石を用いて統一し、明るい南国の息づきを見せている。
LINHOF KARDAN NIKKOR 90mm F4.5 f22 1/8 EPR

1 Katsura Rikyu, "Stepping Stones", Momoyama Era (Kyoto)
The Katsura Rikyu garden in a go-round style displays ideal beauty no matter which portion of it may be cut out. To guide us, the garden is strewn with stepping stones of varied designs. The feel of rock and moss which are well matched with each other, can be said to be an essential element of the Japanese garden.
SINAR P NIKKOR 210mm F5.6 f22 1/15 EPR

2 Katsura Rikyu, "The Front Garden of the Study Room", Momoyama Era (Kyoto)
In a sense the front garden of the study room is the face of Katsura Rikyu. It was built by Prince Tomohito of Hachijo and Prince Tomotada. Even though the building is two generations old, its architectonic beauty was arrived at as a result of the most elaborate calculation of displays for uncomparable perfectness.
SINAR P NIKKOR 90mm F4.5 f22 1/15 EPR

3 Kyoto Imperial Palace, "Osuzumi-sho maenakajima", Edo Era (Kyoto)
The water garden is about 7,000 m^2 wide. The pond near Osuzumisho in the inner garden was designed with emphasis on the stream, accentuated with three islands situated in it. The stepping stones, stone bridge and stone groupings for shore protection compose a landscape full of variety. Together with flowers of each season, they bring about a world of elegance.
SINAR P FUJINON 210mm F5.6 f22 1/15 EPR

4 Shugaku-in Rikyu, "Kami no Chaya", Edo Era (kyoto)
The beauty of the Shugaku-in garden lies in its harmony between grand nature and the artifacts. The spring with its cherry blossoms, the fall blazing with red leaves and the winter with its fluttering snow flakes... Those who visit here in any season will never be disappointed.
LINHOF KARDAN NIKKOR 90mm F4.5 f22 1/15 EPR

5 Shugaku-in Rikyu, "Nishihama at Sunset", Edo Era (Kyoto)
There is no other Japanese garden that incorporates nature as this one does. Nishihama at dusk viewed from the Momijidani area of Kami no Chaya is so dynamic that man-made elements in it are hardly noticeable.
LINHOF KARDAN NIKKOR 90mm F4.5 f16 1/2 EPR

6 Shugaku-in Rikyu, "The Snowy Kami no Chaya", Edo Era (Kyoto)
Shugaku-in under snow displays, even more clearly, the sublime integrity of natural beauty and artificial beauty. Photographing during a heavy snowfall was hard but I was moved by the majestic planning and the superb idea of the ex-Emperor Gomizunoo to have chosen this site and to have designed this garden.
LINHOF KARDAN NIKKOR 90mm F4.5 f8 1/60 EPR

7 Daisen-in, "Karetaki Stone Grouping", Muromachi Era (Kyoto)
The garden is typical of dry landscapes. Steep mountains and deep valleys are expressed in a brief space of only a little more than 100 m^2. The thin line of water streaming out of the depths of the mountain becomes a wide river and flows into the vast ocean. The conception of the flowing, symbolized by white sand, is peculiar to the Japanese garden.
LINHOF KARDAN SYMMAR 150mm F5.6 f22 1/4 EPR

8 Daitoku-ji, "Karetaki Stone Grouping", Edo Era (Kyoto)
Although there are numerous ways of symbolic expression by means of great stones, this dry waterfall expressed with three stones has a gorgeous and mighty composition. The technique was frequently used in the early Edo period. Teishi set at the center represents a watershed stone.
LINHOF KARDAN FUJINON 210mm F5.6 f22 1/4 EPR

9 Sokoku-ji, "Karesansui", Edo Era (Kyoto)
This is a simple, flat-type dry graden suitable for a Zen temple. As a whole, the expression is clear and magnanimous. The stone grouping in the east was partially re-done in the Showa Era. The artificial hill built in the background and the flat space create a double structure effect.
SINAR P SUPERANGULON 75mm F8 f8 1/15 EPR

10 Ryozoku-in, "Karesansui", Edo Era (Kyoto)
Besides streams, large rivers and oceans, the white sand represents such abstract patterns as ripples, swirls or checks. The sand scrolls in this photograph enable the limited space to appear wider and stress the cleanliness.
SINAR P SYMMAR 150mm F5.6 f22 1/15 EPR

11 Ginkaku-ji, "Ginsanada", Muromachi Era (Kyoto)
Yoshimasa Ashikaga had a passion for gardens. One of the features of this garden, designed based on his idea, is Ginsanada (silvery sand sea). When the moon rises above Tsukimachi-yama on the east side, the spreaded sand here ripples with a silvery glint and the Land of Happiness presents itself.
SINAR P NIKKOR 90mm F5.6 f22 1/15 EPR

12 Ryoan-ji, "Karesansui", Muromachi Era (kyoto)
Fifteen stones are scattered in white sand. One may take them as islands on the sea or a hazardous path. This is an adaptable space that has numberless interpretations according to each viewer's mind. It may be called the garden to make viewers philosophize.
LINHOF KARDAN SUPERANGULON 75mm F8 f22 1/8 EPR

13 Saiho-ji, "Moss Garden", Kamakura Era (Kyoto)
Stones, water and mosses are important elements to compose gardens. Particularly famous are mosses of Saiho-ji. When touched by hand, they feel like an infant's skin. Their vivid green in the rainy season is really unforgettable.
LINHOF KARDAN SYMMAR 150mm F5.6 f22 1/8 EPR

14 Saiho-ji, "Around the Island", Kamakura Era (Kyoto)
The garden existed before Muso Kokushi came to live in this temple but its name was changed from Saiho Jodo-ji to Saiho-ji in 1339 when this famous priest and garden designer arrived here. The unearthly atmosphere that fills the entire area stimulates our aspiration for a Pure World away from the secular society.
SINAR P NIKKOR 90mm F4.5 f32 1/2 EPR

15 Sento Imperial Palace, "The Central Part of Chitei", Edo Era (Kyoto)
Like Shugaku-in, this grand water garden is closely related to the ex-Emperor Gomizunoo. The building was started in 1569 under the leadership of Enshu Kobori. The south pond has a sandy beach covered with cobblestones. The exquisitely curved shoreline is even more attractive with varied tints of flowers from season to season.
SINAR P NIKKOR 90mm F4.5 f22 1/15 EPR

16 Tenryu-ji, "Taki Stone Grouping", Kamakura Era (Kyoto)
The area around the waterfall stone grouping in the depths of the garden was designed by Doryu Rankei. The stone bridge, the waterfall stone grouping, Rigyo-seki, Enzan-seki... none of them fails to surprise us with his distinguished ability for artistic formation. This stone grouping, which expresses stirring forcefulness, demonstrates the highest standard of Japanese garden-making technique.
SINAR P FUJINON 210mm F5.6 f22 1/2 EPR

17 Joruri-ji, "A Complete View", Heian Era (Kyoto)
The temple is also called Kutai-ji. On the west bank of the pond, stands Amida-do (Amitabha Hall) in which nine buddhist images are enshrined. The whole area of the pond and the garden were cleaned recently to gain a new aspect. The reflection of Amitabha Hall on the pond never ceases to fascinate us with its rich flavor of the Heian Era.
SINAR P NIKKOR 90mm F4.5 f22 1/4 EPR

18 Kinkaku-ji, "A Complete View", Kamakura Era (Kyoto)
It was built by Yoshimasa Ashikaga. The golden pavillion was burnt down in 1950 and re-constructed in 1955. There are more than ten islands of varied sizes in the pond. The golden reflection on the water looks like a mirage of the prosperous old days.
LINHOF KARDAN NIKKOR 90mm F4.5 f22 1/15 EPR

19 Kinkaku-ji, "Taki Stone Grouping", Kamakura Era (Kyoto)
The stone grouping, as well as that of Tenryu-ji, is superbly composed. Rigyo-seki (carp stone), representing a dragon rising to heaven, is found in the central part where water falls. These stones look as if they are about to move at any moment.
LINHOF KARDAN SYMMAR 150mm F5.6 f22 1/2 EPR

20 Sanpo-in, "Sanzon Stone Grouping", Momoyama Era (Kyoto)
The Sanzon stone grouping is derived from the traditional arrangement of three Buddhist images such as the Amitabha triad with an Amitabha at the center and Kannon and Seshi on both sides of it, or the bhaisajyaguru triad. The central stone of this grouping, called the Fujito stone, was delivered to Sanpo-in by Hideyoshi who inherited it from Nobunaga.
LINHOF KARDAN FUJINON 210mm F5.6 f22 1/8 EPR

21 Nijo-jo, "Gogan Stone Grouping", Momoyama Era (Kyoto)
The castle was built by Ieyasu at this site in 1601. For water gardens, stone grouping for shore protection is almost always an important factor of garden making. Stones selected with utmost care and set by skillful hands breathe and emit light.
LINHOF KARDAN FUJINON 210mm F5.6 f22 1/15 EPR

22 Chijaku-in, "Taki Stone Grouping", Edo Era (Kyoto)
This is the waterfall stone grouping viewed from the northern end of the study room. It somewhat lacks strength when compared to the products of the Kamakura Era but the Edo period surpasses it in elaborateness and delicacy. The form is different from fixed patterns and the expression is free and generous.
LINHOF KARDAN FUJINON 210mm F5.6 f22 1/15 EPR

23 Katsura Rikyu, "Misaki-gata Lantern", Momoyama Era (Kyoto)
There are many shapes of stone lanterns, each of which has its specific name and history. The one in this picture is typical of Misaki-gata lanterns frequently seen in Japanese gardens.
LINHOF KARDAN FUJINON 210mm F5.6 f22 1/15 EPR

24 Shinnyo-in, "Urizane-gata Lantern", Momoyama Era (Kyoto)
The lantern is placed in the Shinnyo-in garden (to be described later). It is made of Muho-to (tomb stone) of the mid-Edo Era with a lamp housing excavated in it. It has an interesting story in that Lord Yoshiaki of the Ashikaga Shogunate named it.
ZENZA BRONICA ZENZANON 150mm F3.5 f16 1/30 EPR

25 Joju-in, "A Complete View", Edo Era (Kyoto)
The adjacent Kiyomizu-dera is a well-known temple which attracts a great many sightseers. Unbelievable silence reigns in the water garden of Joju-in receding from the bustle and noises of Kiyomizu. The pond filled with water is beautiful. Here unfold graceful formations integrated with nature as the borrowed landscape.
LINHOF KARDAN SUPERANGULON 75mm F8 f22 1/15 EPR

26 Honpo-ji, "Karetaki Stone Grouping", Momoyama Era (Kyoto)
This is widely known as a product of Koetsu, a versatile artist particularly famous for pottery, gold-lacquering and calligraphy. The special feature of this dry waterfall is a striped stone, set in the lower portion, meant to represent currents of water. As well as the dry waterfall portion above, it manifests splendid creativity.
LINHOF KARDAN SYMMAR 150mm F5.6 f22 1/2 EPR

27 Shinnyo-in, "A Complete View", Momoyama Era (Kyoto)
The technique to make white sand represent a stream and cobble-stone a sandy beach, was referred to above. Besides, in this garden scale-like stones are used to symbolize a large river. It's dynamic and magnificent. The garden-making characteristic one of the Momoyama Era is plainly known for that.
LINHOF KARDAN NIKKOR 90mm F4.5 f22 1/8 EPR

28 Manshu-in, "Ishibashi Stone Grouping", Edo Era (Kyoto)
What attracts visitors to this garden first is this stone bridge. Bridge stones are grouped conspicuously high in the back of the central area and a mountain stream flows under them. The composition inspires a magnanimous mood which indicates the garden designer's ability.
LINHOF KARDAN FUJINON 210mm F5.6 f22 1/8 EPR

29 Nishi Hongan-ji, "Kame Stone Grouping", Edo Era (Kyoto)
The approximately 760 m^2 wide garden, also known as "the Kokei no Niwa," includes a dry waterfall, two stone bridges, a powerful watershed stone, crane and tortoise stone groupings. Japanese sago palms were planted following the fashion of the time. The assiduously-made landscape can be said to be the masterpiece of Japanese gardens.
LINHOF KARDAN FUJINON 210mm F5.6 f22 1/15 EPR

30 Konchi-in, "Tsuru Stone Grouping", Edo Era (Kyoto)
A worship stone is placed at the center beyond the white sand which spreads, curving gently, in the front. The crane island on the right and the tortoise island on the left are the main features of this garden. They give a sense of grandeur and brightness. The Tsurukubi-ishi (crane neck stone) is particularly majestic.
LINHOF KARDAN NIKKOR 90mm F4.5 f22 1/15 EPR

31 Ikkyu-ji, "Karesansui at the East Garden", Edo Era (Kyoto)
Sojun Ikkyu built his own grave in this temple while he was living. He died here in 1481. The temple has four gardens: the front garden of the graveyard, the south garden, the north garden and the east garden. The east garden, called "the garden of 16 disciples of Buddha," is filled with air worthy of the name of a Zen temple.
LINHOF KARDAN FUJINON 120mm F8 f22 1/8 EPR

32 Reiun-in, "A Complete View", Muromachi Era (Kyoto)
This garden of Reiun-in, a minor temple belonging to Myoshin-ji, has strong characteristic traits. What is signified by the stones radially arranged around a boulder as the center in this small garden of only about 60 m^2? The ample voluminousness is strong and exciting. It appeals to viewers strongly.
LINHOF KARDAN NIKKOR 90mm F4.5 f32 1/2 EPR

33 Nanzen-ji, "A Complete View", Edo Era (Kyoto)
The neighborhood of Nanzen-ji is famous for its scenic beauty, even in Kyoto. The stone grouping surrounded by white sand is set extremely close to the mud wall. The method, also adapted in the garden Daitoku-ji Honbo, is characteristic of the time.
SINAR P NIKKOR 90mm F4.5 f22 1/15 EPR

34 Tokai-an, "A Complete View of the Courtyard", Edo Era (Kyoto)
This garden is the narrowest and smallest of all the gardens shown here. It is a dry landscape with a total dimension of 41.25 m^2. The stone arranged in a straight line are full of variety. The space partitioned by a connecting corridor is filled with a crisp and tense feeling. It was made by Toboku Osho in 1814.
SINAR P NIKKOR 90mm F4.5 f22 1/8 EPR

35 Omote Senke, "Around the Zangetsu-tei" Momoyama Era (Kyoto)
Sho-an, Senno Rikyu's son, re-established the Sen family after his father comitted harakiri. The garden is adjacent to such tea houses as Fushin-an, Zangetsu-tei and Tensetsu-do. The plantations which are meticulously cared for by hand, give rise to secluded air and invite visitors to an ultramundane world.
LINHOF KARDAN SUPERANGULON 75mm F8 f22 1/2 EPR

36 Ura Senke, "At the Yuin", Edo Era (Kyoto)
Ura Senke was founded by Genpaku Sotan, a grandchild of Senno Rikyu. There are a number of tea houses, including Konnichi-an, Yuin, Kanun-tei, Mushiki-ken, Totsutotsu-sai, Hosen-sai, and Tairyu-ken in the garden, which are highly evaluated by educated people as the culmination of wabi, taste for the simple and quiet.
LINHOF KARDAN SUPERANGULON 75mm F8 f22 1/2 EPR

37 Mushanokoji Senke, "At the Middle Gate", Edo Era (Kyoto)
Ichio Soshu, the second son of Sotan, built Kankyu-an at the present Mushanokoji Ogawa Higashi when he retired. This photograph is a portion of the garden's middle gate. The Amigasa gate, with a rustic shingle roof, is suggestive of a tasteful hut. It relaxes us.
LINHOF KARDAN SUPERANGULON 75mm F8 f22 1/2 EPR

38 Yabunouchi Soke, "Around the Machiai", Edo Era (Kyoto)
Shochi Tsuruginaka, the founder, served Oda Nobunaga as an attendant in charge of tea ceremony. Together with the three Sen families, he contributed much to the development of the art mainly through the establishment of the Shoin (study room) style tea ceremony. In this Machiai, too, seats for peers are separated from those for ordinary guests.
LINHOF KARDAN SUPERANGULON 75mm F8 f22 1/4 EPR

39 Koho-an, "Sanunjo Tsukubai", Edo Era (Kyoto)
The Bosen tea room of Koho-an is one of the most prominent of all tea rooms. The Sanunjo shown here is a hermitage-like garden. The water basin is called Fusen-no-Tsukubai. Enshu Kobori created it hoping to develop the art of ceremonial tea-making.
LINHOF KARDAN FUJINON 120mm F8 f16 1/2 EPR

40 Omote Senke, "Fushin-an Tsukubai", Momoyama Era (Kyoto)
Omote Senke's tea garden is the extremity of simplicity and quietness. The garden forms an unearthly world into which a landscape of deep mountains and gorges appears to have been condensed. This water basin is of air suitable for the garden. It expresses both practical beauty and beauty of form.
LINHOF KARDAN FUJINON 120mm F8 f22 1 EPR

41 Mushanokoji Senke, "Kankyu-an Tsukubai", Edo Era (Kyoto)
This type of water basin was made by using the body of a Hokyoin-type (square) stone tower or a multi-story stone tower. Each of the four sides has a buddhist image relief. Known as Shiho-butsu (four-side buddha) no Tsukubai, fine articles of this type are widely used in famous tea houses and tea gardens.
LINHOF KARDAN SYMMAR 150mm F5.6 f22 1/2 EPR

42 Shojuraigo-ji, "A Water Basin", Momoyama Era (Shiga)
The temple situated at the eastern foot of Mt. Hiei was founded by Eshin Sozu. The top of a stone tower made in the mid-Kamakura Era was placed upside down on a cylindrical shaft for use as a water basin. It has another name, "Nichigetsu no Chozubachi" (water basin of the sun and moon). The massive voluminousness is beautiful.
LINHOF KARDAN FUJINON 210mm F5.6 f22 1/4 EPR

43 Tokai-an, "Ichimonji Water Basin", Edo Era (Kyoto)
It was named after its drain hole which is curved in the shape of a short, straight line. Guests wash their mouths and hands while stooping by the Tsukubai as seen in Omote Senke's and the Kankyu-an tea gardens, but these water basins are used for washing while standing. They are also called Ensaki (edge of verandah) Chozubachi.
LINHOF KARDAN FUJINON 210mm F5.6 f22 1/4 EPR

44 Katsura Rikyu, "Katsura-gaki", Momoyama Era (Kyoto)
Japan has abundant bamboo, which is frequently used for tea houses and Sukiya-style buildings. This bamboo fence is the enclosure erected on the left side of the Katsura Rikyu entrance. The classical design is pleasant. It indicates a boundary between the clergy and the laity.
LINHOF KARDAN SYMMAR 150mm F5.6 f22 1/8 EPR

45 Kinkaku-ji, "Kinkakuji-gaki", Kamakura Era (Kyoto)
This is a kind of enclosure fence and a variation of Yotsume-gaki (four-eyed fence). For ordinary Yotsume-gaki, horizontal bamboo on the top, as seen in this picture, are not used. The fence is low and the bamboo is arranged spaced widely apart. The plain, rustic sense is loved by masters of Cha-no-yu.
LINHOF KARDAN FUJINON 120mm F8 f22 1/8 EPR

46 Koho-an, "Yarai-gaki", Edo Era (Kyoto)
This bamboo fence is erected around the entrance and the stone bridge of Koho-an. It has manly architectonic beauty. Characterized by ends of strong and sturdy bamboo sharpened like spear heads, the fence shows an attitude of candid refusal.
LINHOF KARDAN SYMMAR 150mm F5.6 f22 1/4 EPR

47 Yabunouchi Soke, "Teppo-gaki", Edo Era (Kyoto)
Bamboo, with a diameter of a little more than 12cm, is split lengthwise and bundled. The bundles, tied with hemp palm rope to intertwine them, are stood alternately in the back and front of the horizontal frame. The mild and gentle air of Yabunouchi Soke's tea garden does not have anything rejectional about it as expressed by Yarai-gaki.
LINHOF KARDAN SYMMAR 150mm F5.6 f22 1/8 EPR

48 Mr. Seido's Seibi-en Garden, "Taki Stone Grouping", Meiji Era (Aomori)
Bugaku Oishi, who had actively engaged in garden-making in Edo, visited Aomori and supervised a number of garden-makings. Thus, gardens of his style were in fashion in this northern part of Japan. This garden was made by Teiji Obata, one of his disciples. The technique, which was developed in the early Edo period, is found everywhere in accurate groupings of stones.
LINHOF KARDAN FUJINON 210mm F5.6 f22 1/8 EPR

49 Motsu-ji, "Nakajima Stone Grouping", Heian Era (Iwate)
Most gardens made in the Heian Era were with large ponds, but only this temple has a pond in which a Shumisen-style stone grouping is laid. When it was erected, it is said that there were three palatial buildings and an arch bridge of about 21m long to visualize the Pure Land.
LINHOF KARDAN SYMMAR 150mm F5.6 f22 1/8 EPR

50 Yosan-ji, "Ookarikomi at the Central Part", Momoyama Era (Akita)
Raikyu-ji, Daichi-ji and Jiko-in are a few of the temples famous for their little leaf boxes. Above all, this temple's leaf box is large in scale. Big waves and ripples are expressed by it. Although the layout is different, it brings back memories of Raikyu-ji. Gardens with leaf boxes are rare in the Tohoku district.
LINHOF KARDAN SYMMAR 150mm F5.6 f22 1/8 EPR

51 Gyokusen-ji, "A Complete View", Edo Era (Yamagata)
The principal feature of this garden, made behind the study room, is the pond. A cascade falls from the hillside and three islands are laid in the pond. The trees in the background are thick and in perfect harmony with nature. Stones are laid sharply and forcefully in even detail. The overall view is dynamic and enchanting.
LINHOF KARDAN FUJINON 120mm F8 f22 1/8 EPR

52 Rinno-ji, "The Central Island", Edo Era (Tochigi)
The scale is great with Mt. Nantai and the main building of Rinno-ji as borrowed landscape. The pond stretching from east to west, occupies an area of 3,158 m^2. Azaleas are planted beautifully. The Kanto district has few fine gardens, but this one is one of the best of those few.
LINHOF KARDAN NIKKOR 90mm F4.5 f22 1/8 EPR

53 Nonin-ji, "Taki Stone Grouping, Edo Era (Saitama)
This is the only famous garden in Saitama Prefecture. The water garden, which makes use of its hillside location, is meticulously maintained. The waterfall stone grouping on the right hillside is powerful and gorgeous. The cave stone grouping, stone bridge, stone grouping for shore protection and other stone works are fine examples of the art of the time.
LINHOF KARDAN FUJINON 210mm F5.6 f22 1/8 EPR

54 Kencho-ji, "A Complete View", Edo Era (Kanagawa)
The temple was opened by Daikaku Zenji in 1253. As there are lots of cultural assets in the precincts, sightseers keep visiting this temple. Despite the din and bustle, the garden gives a tidy and subdued appearance. Deep plantations, well balanced with it, express modest beauty even though the garden has no eye-catching stone grouping.
LINHOF KARDAN NIKKOR 90mm F4.5 f22 1/8 EPR

55 Kyu Shiba Rikyu, "The Central Part of Chitei" Edo Era (Tokyo)
The garden suffered severe war damage but regained its original, beautiful figure through the metropolitan government's restoration work after the war. The Chinese-style bridge connecting the island creates an exotic mood. A stone grouping of the Edo Era remains on the hillside of the island.
LINHOF KARDAN NIKKOR 90mm F4.5 f22 1/8 EPR

56 Choraku-ji, "Chitei and Tsukiyama", Edo Era (Shizuoka)
Because nearly 100 dodan azalea trees are planted on a man-made hill at the foot of the mountain, the garden is also called "Dodan no Niwa." The garden, ascribed to Enshu Kobori, is representative of this part of Japan. The view, which incorporates the surrounding nature, is magnificent.
LINHOF KARDAN NIKKOR 90mm F4.5 f22 1/8 EPR

57 Manko-ji, "Sanzon Stone Grouping", Edo Era (Aichi)
The garden is in the backyard of the priests' quarters and is surrounded by thick growths of natural forest. The artificial hill is almost entirely covered with varied stone groupings of a waterfall, Horai-san and Sanzon. The sublime appearance is overwhelming.
LINHOF KARDAN FUJINON 210mm F5.6 f22 1/8 EPR

58 Erin-ji, "Taki Stone Grouping", Kamakura Era (Yamanashi)
This temple is noted for the words: "Clear your mind of all mundane thoughts, and you will find even fire cool." The oldest portion is the Shumisen stone grouping on an upper part of the miniature hill. The other portions were repaired by the orders of Ieyasu, Yoshiyasu and other patrons. With refined technique found everywhere, this can be said to be a garden made adroitly.
LINHOF KARDAN FUJINON 210mm F5.6 f22 1/8 EPR

59 Daizen-ji, "Tsukiyama Shudan Stone Grouping", Edo Era (Yamanashi)
The Bhaisajyaguru image, to which the temple is dedicated, is a national treasure. It is also called "Budo Yakushi". The establishment of this prominent temple is attributed to Gyoki. On the left side miniature hill, a Shumisen-style stone grouping and a Tsurushima-style stone grouping co-exist. The method, indicative of manly strength, is well worth our viewing.
LINHOF KARDAN FUJINON 210mm F5.6 f32 1/4 EPR

60 Jizo-ji, "A Complete View", Edo Era (Nagano)
A subtle and profound atmosphere prevails in this garden which was built southeast of the study room behind the main building by making use of limpid spring water. The beauty is doubled by a reflection on the water of thick and heavy growths which were planted following a deep and complex ground plan.
LINHOF KARDAN NIKKOR 90mm F4.5 f22 1/4 EPR

61 Eihou-ji, "Bonnongan Falls", Kamakura Era (Gifu)
Muso Kokushi, a distinguished priest in the Kamakura Era, established this temple. The Kaizan-do building has been designated as a national treasure. On the west side of the pond parted by the Musai bridge, the Bonnongan waterfall is located. The sound of water falling to the bright garden fascinates viewers with its feeling of pureness.
LINHOF KARDAN SYMMAR 150mm F5.6 f22 1/8 EPR

62 Kenroku-en, "Kotoji-gata Lantern", Edo Era (Ishikawa)
Kenroku-en, a famous garden of a feudal lord, was built during the time of Lord Toshinaga, the second chief of the Maeda clan who reigned the one million-Koku Kaga fief. An attraction of this wide garden is this Kotoji-gata (bridge-shape of a Japanese harp) lantern. It is found at the very beginning of the sightseeing course. Tourists swarm there to take snap shots.
LINHOF KARDAN SYMMAR 150mm F5.6 f22 1/8 EPR

63 Rinno-ji, "Multi-story Stone Tower", Edo Era (Tochigi)
It is placed on the island in the Rinno-ji garden of Nikko. Full-scale multi-story towers are erected for the repose of the dead but those for use in gardens function as items to enhance the beauty of the pond rather than for lighting purposes.
LINHOF KARDAN NIKKOR 500mm F8 f22 1/4 EPR

64 Rakuraku-en, "Daikaku-gata Lantern", Era Unspecified (Shiga)
The lantern is used for various practical purposes such as lighting, offerings to a god, repose of the dead and decoration. This lantern is set on an artificial hill. There is a bridge on the left side of it and a garden path below it. The lantern serves both for lighting and as an additional item. Today, it is mostly regarded as an added item.
LINHOF KARDAN FUJINON 210mm F5.6 f22 1/8 EPR

65 Koraku-en, "Hotaru-gata Lantern", Edo Era (Okayama)
There are only a few thin drum-like lanterns. A hook is provided in the upper portion of the lamp housing to fix the lantern when it's hung. They must have been used frequently since they were installed along the stream flowing toward the Enyo-tei.
MAMIYA R.Z. SEKOR 180mm F4.5 f16 1/15 EPR

66 Kenroku-en, "Seisonkaku Tea Garden", Edo Era (Ishikawa)
This was built as a retreat for Takako, the wife of the 12th Lord Narihiro of the one million-Koku Maeda clan. A winding-water type tea garden like this is rarely seen. Being snow country, a unique composition with stepping stones laid inside the eaves was used.
LINHOF KARDAN FUJINON 120mm F8 f22 1/2 EPR

67 Seisui-en, "Taki Stone Grouping", Edo Era (Niigata)
This is a go-round style water garden. The pond has a headland on the east side. Its rugged shore is assumed to have been made consciously of Katsura Rikyu. A Misaki-gata lantern is placed at the end of the headland. The garden belonged to the suburban residences of the Mizoguchi family, the lord of the Shibata fief. The beautiful plantations enhance the tasteful appearance of high tone.
LINHOF KARDAN SYMMAR 150mm F5.6 f22 1/4 EPR

68 The Site of Mr. Asakura's Residence, "Suwakan Ato Stone Grouping", Momoyama Era (Fukui)
The garden has manly and powerful stone groupings of the Momoyama Era remaining at the sites of Suwa-kan, as shown in this photograph, of Oyudono (the bath house), and of Nanyo-ji. Boulders standing in this garden, meant to represent a waterless cascade and concurrently Horai, the legendary Isle of Eternal Youth, are of overwhelmingly strong appeal to viewers.
LINHOF KARDAN FUJINON 210mm F5.6 f22 1/2 EPR

69 Kenroku-en, "The Island of Chitei", Edo Era (Ishikawa)
The water garden comprises two parts: the upper Kasumigaike and the lower Hyoike. The original garden was somewhat different from the present one as some work was done on it between the earlier and latter days of the Edo period. The crystal stream flowing out of Mt. Yamazaki runs through the garden, winding and swirling.
LINHOF KARDAN FUJINON 210mm F5.6 f22 1/2 EPR

70 Saimyo-ji, "A Complete View", Edo Era (Shiga)
The establishment of Saimyo-ji, one of the three temples on the east side of Lake Biwa, dates back to the Heian Era. The water garden in the backyard of the main building was reduced in scale due to damage caused by repeated floods. Nonetheless, the stone groupings of a dry waterfall and the Isle of Eternal Youth on the hillside show us the beauty still intact from the time of their establishment.
LINHOF KARDAN NIKKOR 90mm F4.5 f22 1/4 EPR

71 Daichi-ji, "A Complete View", Edo Era (Shiga)
The great leaf box of Sanbo represents a surge of the sea and the boat-like leaf box on the front left signifies a treasure ship. There is a surprisingly large number of gardens in Shiga Prefecture as is known from the fact that it is called a treasure house of stone arts or fine gardens. This temple is one example with its strong identity.
LINHOF KARDAN SYMMAR 150mm F5.6 f22 1/8 EPR

72 Kitabatake-jinja, "Gogan Stone Grouping", Muromachi Era (Mie)
Originally, this was the garden of the residence of Governor Kitabatake but was later made into a shrine. In this water garden, with its winding stream style, stone groupings are seen from place to place and the spirit of the time which valued simplicity and fortitude, is keenly sensed. Particularly, the dry landscape arranged under the sacred tree is full of vigor.
LINHOF KARDAN FUJINON 120mm F8 f22 1/2 EPR

73 Enman-in, "A Complete View", Edo Era (Shiga)
This is one of the temples affiliated with Onjo-ji Mii-dera which is famous for "the evening bell of the Mii Temple." It is believed to have been founded by Enchin. There are two islands representing a crane and a tortoise in the front garden of the main building. The dry waterfall and shore protections are gracefully made to harmonize with cherry blossoms in spring and crimson foliage in autumn, giving the garden an elegant aspect.
LINHOF KARDAN SYMMAR 150mm F5.6 f22 1/8 EPR

74 Fumon-in, "Karetaki Stone Grouping", Edo Era (Wakayama)
There are a number of temples on Mt. Koya which is famous for its founder, Kobo Daishi. Fumon-in is one of them. The garden looks expansive, with the Kameshima, tortoise island, in the north connected by two stone bridges. Many tourists are attracted to this place which is cool in summer. It is hidden in dimness in winter, however, as the snow prohibits anyone from approaching it.
LINHOF KARDAN FUJINON 210mm F5.6 f32 1/2 EPR

75 Negoro-ji, "Taki Stone Grouping", Edo Era (Wakayama)
The garden is in the north part of the study room. The three-step cascade is made on a hillside and a stone to represent a background mountain is set beyond it. The pond is made with two islands, Tsurushima and Kameshima, and two stone bridges. They suggest a refined technique. In addition, a cave and a Yodomari-ishi are formed. The overall landscape is beautiful. The garden is well worth seeing.
LINHOF KARDAN FUJINON 210mm F5.6 f32 1/2 EPR

76 Tentoku-in, "Karetaki Stone Grouping", Momoyama Era (Wakayama)
The temple is the oldest and has the clearest historic record among those within the precincts of Mt. Koya. It was built in 1622 for the salvation of the desparted soul of Lady Toshitsune Maeda, the wife of the Lord of Kaga. The garden looks somewhat unkept but the dry waterfall in Sanzon style shown here is most impressive because of the sublime arrangement of stones.
LINHOF KARDAN FUJINON 210mm F5.6 f32 1/2 EPR

77 Hokke-ji, "A Complete View", Edo Era (Nara)
This is a nunnery established by Empress Komyo. The principal image, a wood carving of Juichimen Kannon (Ekadasamukha), which is said to have been modeled after the empress hereself, is a masterpiece of the Heian Era. The lovely pond is equipped with a sod bridge and the bed of the stream is covered with small stones. The graceful air is befitting for a nunnery.
LINHOF KARDAN NIKKOR 90mm F4.5 f22 1/8 EPR

78 Gangyo-ji, "A Complete View", Momoyama Era (Nara)
Mt. Yoshino, famous for cherry blossoms, is close to the temple and is thronged with cherry blossom viewers during the season. The waterless portion of the pond is filled with cobblestone and the miniature hill has a Horai stone grouping. The cave stone grouping arranged in a bridge-like form is a focal point of this garden. The limited space is bright and clear and gives a crisp and strained feeling.
LINHOF KARDAN NIKKOR 90mm F4.5 f22 1/8 EPR

79 Raikyu-ji, "Tsurushima and Ookarikomi", Momoyama Era (Okayama)
Enshu Kobori made this garden sometime around 1604, the year of his appointment as the lord of Matsuyama Castle. There is no garden like this made with the audacious idea of expressing the surge of the sea by using nothing but a little leaf box. The abstract composition is fascinating. Personally, I prefer flowerless views of this garden to those during the flower season.
LINHOF KARDAN SYMMAR 150mm F5.6 f22 1/8 EPR

80 Koraku-en, "The Central Part of the Chitei", Edo Era (Okayama)
There is an artificial hill called Yuishinzan at the center of the garden. The top of the hill is the best spot to view from but the angle of this picture, with Okayama Castle seen in the distance, is worth trying. Stone groupings, a winding stream, a zigzag bridge, an arbor, Enyo-tei and other features are scattered nicely. The garden is full of things which are a pleasure to see.
LINHOF KARDAN NIKKOR 90mm F4.5 f22 1/15 EPR

81 Mr. Fukada's Private Garden, "Stone Bridge and Sanzon Stone Grouping", Kamakura Era (Tottori)
The Fukadas are a historic family as is illustrated by the fact that Emperor Godaigo's temporary quarters was made here when he was transferred to Oki Island. It is miraculous that a garden of that age has been privately inherited over hundreds of years to this day. The Sanzon stone grouping and the Tsurukame stone grouping are impressive enough.
LINHOF KARDAN NIKKOR 90mm F4.5 f22 1/2 EPR

82 Shukkei-en, "The Island and the Stone Bridge," Momoyama Era (Hiroshima)
It was severely damaged by the atomic bomb in August 1945, but was re-constructed to it original state six years later. The garden was designed by Soko Ueda, a master of ceremonial tea. The go-round style garden has various scenic spots including a miniature hill, a sandy beach, a gorge and a waterfall. Its beauty which changes in accordance with the advance of the seasons is most delightful.
LINHOF KARDAN FUJINON 210mm F5.6 f22 1/8 EPR

83 Iko-ji, "Kameshima", Muromachi Era (Shimane)
Sesshu, a great master of painting, made this garden when he was invited by Lord Masuda to come and live in this temple. The shape of the Kameshima, the island, is realistic and easy to recognize. It is full of movement as if it were ready to move at any moment. The garden displays its charm to the fullest extent when drooping cherry trees on the hillside are in bloom.
LINHOF KARDAN SYMMAR 150mm F5.6 f22 1/8 EPR

84 Mr. Ogawa's Private Garden, "A Complete View", Muromachi Era (Shimane)
The Ogawa family dominated this region in the early Muromachi Era and was respectfully called Wagi Shogun. The shore protection and the dry waterfall at the foot of the hill indicate the skillful construction as well as the finest choice of stone materials. Above all, the dry waterfall in the central part still exists. It is one of the attractions of this garden.
LINHOF KARDAN NIKKOR 90mm F4.5 f22 1/8 EPR

85 Mr. Katsura's Private Garden, "A Complete View", Edo Era (Yamaguchi)
The garden gives a strange impression beyond expression. Of numerous stone gardens throughout the country, this is the most peculiar one. Here, stones are laid over other stones rather than arranged as a group. The technique was used only in this garden, which was given the name of "Tsuki no Katsura".
LINHOF KARDAN NIKKOR 90mm F4.5 f22 1/8 EPR

86 Ritsurin-en, "The Island", Edo Era (Kagawa)
The park with a dimension of 759,000 m^2 is varied by 1.5 million people a year. The forest of Japanese red pines and black pines, the most remarkable feature there, is quite impressive. Apart from the care needed to maintain them, the weight of the 230-year history fascinates us.
LINHOF KARDAN FUJINON 210mm F5.6 f22 1/8 EPR

87 Ritsurin-en, "A Complete View", Edo Era (kagawa)
This photograph was taken from Hirai-ho. Backed by magnificent Shiunzan, the view of Engetsu-kyo, Sei-ko and Kikugetsu-tei is beautiful and stirring. The garden is so spacious that it takes about half a day to go through the six ponds and the 13 artificial hills in it. It can be said to be one of the finest gardens in Japan.
LINHOF KARDAN FUJINON 120mm F8 f22 1/8 EPR

88 Kenroku-en, "Gangyo Stone Bridge", Edo Era (Ishikawa)
The stream flowing through the garden was made by using the abundant spring water available. In the photographed area, the stream, following a winding course, is shallow and transparent. The stone bridge, made of slabs in a tortoise shell shape arranged like a flock of flying wild geese, is unique to this garden and is widely known.
LINHOF KARDAN SYMMAR 150mm F5.6 f22 1/8 EPR

89 Koraku-en, "Yatsuhashi", Edo Era (Okayama)
There are many kinds of Yatsuhashi. They differ in materials such as stone, sod or wood, and are laid using a variety of methods. This one is of a simple make, with boards arranged alternately, and serves to give variety to the landscape in the front.
LINHOF KARDAN SYMMAR 150mm F5.6 f22 1/8 EPR

90 Tamon-ji, "Taki Stone Grouping", Kamakura Era (Tokushima)
Shikoku has many fine gardens. Particularly, Tokushima is provided with gardens which display wonderful formative skills. This may have some connection with the historic fact that Awa Aoishi (Blue Stone of Awa) has been produced here since long time ago. The mighty, heavy-boned stone grouping looks as if it is about to jump out of the small site.
LINHOF KARDAN FUJINON 210mm F5.6 f22 1/4 EPR

91 Gansho-ji, "A Complete View", Kamakura Era (Tokushima)
Like that of Tamon-ji, this is a small garden. The view around the waterfall stone grouping is almost identical to Ryumon-baku of Tenryu-ji. The gorgeousness is made complete with Enzan-seki and Rigyo-seki which attract attention. Formerly, water must have fell but it is waterless now and the pond below is dry, too.
LINHOF KARDAN NIKKOR 90mm F4.5 f22 1/4 EPR

92 Hokoku-ji, "A Complete View", Muromachi Era (Ehime)
A go-round style water garden, of which plots of land are interestingly complicated with stone groupings everywhere. The dry waterfall, in bold style, in the central part is typical of the time. This kind of garden is favored by the experts. The careful maintenance to make the stones be viewed clearly by intentionally doing away with plantations is pleasing.
LINHOF KARDAN FUJINON 120mm F8 f22 1/4 EPR

93 Sennyo-ji, "Around the Island", Edo Era (Fukuoka)
Formally called Raisan Sennyo-ji Daihi **Ouin,** this is a great temple that had 300 houses of monks at one time. The garden in front of the study room, surrounded by secluded forest, is particularly beautiful in autumn when the leaves turn color. The stone grouping looks unattended but the quiet air around the two islands makes viewers feel very peaceful.
LINHOF KARDAN NIKKOR 90mm F4.5 f22 1/2 EPR

94 Mr. Mori's Private Garden, "Taki Stone Grouping", Edo Era (Kagoshima)
Chiran-cho, where Mr. Mori's garden is situated, was a commando base of the former Imperial Navy. In this area, residences of higher-ranked Samurai stand side by side, each with a garden of dry landscape which is thronged with sightseers. Among them, only Mr. Mori's garden is a water garden. The stone grouping reminds us of gardens of Okinawa.
LINHOF KARDAN FUJINON 210mm F5.6 f22 1/4 EPR

95 Suizen-ji, "A Complete View", Edo Era (Kumamoto)
The area is rich with spring water. The miniature hill molded after Mt. Fuji mirrored on the crystal clear water gives a strong impression to visitors. Tadatoshi Hosokawa had the garden-making started in 1637. There are three islands in the south and north and they are connected through dales.
LINHOF KARDAN NIKKOR 90mm F4.5 f22 1/8 EPR

96 Mr. Ishigaki's Private Garden, "A Complete View", Edo Era (Okinawa)
Although the main island of Okinawa was totally devastated during the war, Ishigaki Island narrowly escaped war damage. The existing garden is of value as a reference when considering the lost gardens of the main island. It was made by Unjo Machika, a gardener from Shuri. Kaishoku-seki used in the stone grouping on the artificial hill and in other places gives an integrated impression and expresses the breathing of a southern country full of brightness.
LINHOF KARDAN NIKKOR 90mm F4.5 f22 1/8 EPR

あとがき

はじめ報道写真を志ざした私が，庭の写真を撮り続けて，かれこれ三十年になる。そのきっかけは，現写真評論家・重森弘淹氏から氏の父君重森三玲先生（庭園研究家）を紹介されたのが最初だった。

初対面の庭は，京都東福寺山内光明禅院庭園だった。三日程通い続けて作品らしいものを作り，見て頂くと，黒い写真ですねぇーとの一言(当時はモノクロ写真)だった。暗部はつぶれ，ハイライト部分が素っ飛んだ主観性の強い個性のある写真だったようだ。この黒い写真の一言を理解するのに長い時間を費した。滝石組とか，三尊石組，遠山石とかいった大事な石組は，大抵樹木におおわれた光のささない暗い所にあるのが多い。当時の私はどれが三尊なのか滝石組なのか知る由もない。さんさんと輝く陽光の中，白砂がきらめき巨石が黒くうずくまる。こうした光景を目前にした私は夢中でシャッターを切った。それが黒い写真なのだ。そこには輝く白砂と黒い岩塊が写っているだけなのだ。年月がたつにつれ庭の持っている約束事，つまり石組とか，地割とか，飛石とかその約束事が写っていなければならない，庭を構成する要素・素材を理解しない限り庭の写真とはいえないことが分かってきた。特に露地にいたっては約束事の固まりといっていい。躙口，蹲踞，中門，飛石，役石，燈籠等どれを取っても作者の意図・意味がある。茶室内部にいたっては現在も勉強中という所ではほとんどお手上げという状態が続いている。

そんな事を何も知らなかった私の写真が黒いだけだったのも当り前，とにかく庭の写真ではないのである。良い写真だなぁーと褒め言葉を頂けるようになったのは先生の作品を撮り始めた頃だと思う。良い庭，悪い庭の区別がつき始めた。庭を理解し始めたといっていい。しかしそれでも充分ではなく撮り直しが続いた。はじめはやさしかった先生も年を追うごとに手きびしくなってきた。写真に注文がつき出したのだ。狭い局部から広い視野で，広い視野から狭い局部へと，私は狭い局部で徹底して石組のなんたるかを仕込まれたのだ。今思うとこれは時代を判別する上で一つの手だてとしての教えであったと思う。先生も御自分で写真を撮られていたから，教え方も知っていたのだ。有難いと思う。

花を撮っている写真家にこんな話を聞いたことがある。一つの花を撮る時，おしべが何本，めしべがどんな形をしているか，また花弁が何枚か，さらに欲を言えば葉の形がどのようについているかが，写しこまれている写真がよいという。花名が分かるし，植種も分かるし由来も分かるというからだ。その話を聞いた時，庭の写真に似ているな，と思った。そんな時グラフィック社の赤平覚三氏から写真集を，との話が舞い込んだ。四季の庭ということだったので色々と四季を選んで見たがどうも納得が行かない。花鳥風月的な写真は撮っていないし思いあぐんでいるうち，改めて庭が写真集，作品集になり得るのかという疑問にぶつかった。庭の場合，庭そのものが作品であるし，何百年もの間完成された美を持ち続け，叡智をかたむけた作庭家が存在しているのだ。そんな対象にカメラを向けてシャッターを切る，所詮複写ではないのか？先人達の庭の写真は，仏像は，建築は……と。しかし，私の選んだアングルや角度は，私自身のものであることには違いない。そう，これでいい，これで行こうそして選んだのがこれらの写真である。

手解きを受けた三玲先生はもうこの世にはいない。その教えが私の中にどう生かされているかとくと見て頂きたいと思う。諸兄の御高評を賜わりたいと思う。終りに，序文を寄稿して下さった草野心平先生，お口添へを頂いた重森弘淹氏，デザイナーの熊谷博人氏，そしてこの本の企画・進行を担当下さったグラフィック社の赤平覚三氏の方々に厚く御礼申し上げると共に地下に眠られている三玲先生に見て欲しいと思う。　合掌

1985年11月

大橋治三

AFTERWORD

Initially aspiring to be a news photographer, I have taken pictures of gardens for over approximately 30 years. It all began when I was introduced to Master Mirei Shigemori (a landscape researcher) by his son, Mr. Koen Shigemori, a photograph critic today.

The first garden was the Sandai Komyozenin Garden at the Tofuku-ji Temple in Kyoto. When I showed Master Shigemori some feasibly acceptable photographs I had taken after commuting to the garden for 3 days, he said. "They're black pictures, aren't they?" (Pictures at that period were monochrome.) The Pictures had strong subjective characteristics where the dark areas were blurred and the highlighted areas appeared to jump out. It took me awhile to comprehend what he meant by them being black pictures. The leading stone groupings such as the Taki, Sanzon, and Enzan group of stones were frequently located in dark sites shaded by large bushes and shrubs. At that time I had no reason to know which was the Sanzon or the Taki. As the white sand shone brilliantly in the sunlight, the gigantic rocks appeared black and crouching. Absorbed in the sight before me I became engrossed with snapping the shutter. They had become black pictures. Only the sparkling white sand and black masses of rocks were pictured.

As time went by I made a pledge to myself. I had to somehow capture the stone groupings, the plots of ground, the stepping stones, and other details in my pictures. I came to understand that as long as I remained ignorant of the elements and materials that composed a garden, I could never truly call them pictures of gardens. You could say I was intent on depicting the bare ground, in particular.

Whatever the intentions of the photographer whether he may take pictures of the entrance to the tearoom, stone wash basins, central gate, stepping stone, yakuishi, stone lanterns, etc., there is significance and meaning in them. Photographers have almost given up on photographing places like the interior of tea ceremony rooms which are under study. Unaware of these things, it is not surprising that my photos appeared primarily black; they were not photographs of gardens. From this experience I began striving to photograph Master Shigemori's works in hopes of receiving his praises. Learning to distinguish good gardens from bad ones, I started to understand what a garden was. However, this itself was insufficient and I retook one picture after another. Master Shigemori who was lenient in the beginning became stricter with each passing year giving out directives on the pictures which involved moving from narrow localized areas to broader views and vice versa. Focusing on narrow localized areas, I was taught every detail concerning the essence of stone grouping. Reflecting back, this is one way of teaching that distinguished the period. Because Master Shigemori also took photographs himself, I could understand his teachings. I am indebted to him.

I have heard this from photographers specializing in flowers. When portraying on flower, one must know the name of the flower, the species as well as the origin in addition to knowing the number of stamens, the shape of pistils, the number of petals and more circumstantially the shape of the leaves in order to produce a good picture incorporating all these elements. When I heard this, I thought how it resembled taking pictures of gardens.

At this time I had an offer to do a photo collection from Mr. Kakuzo Akahira of Graphic-sha Publishing Co., Ltd. The theme was to be on gardens through the seasons, however, I could not select among the various seasons anything to satisfy me. I was at loss at the pictures taken were not natural scenic ones. Again, I ran into the problem as to whether the gardens could be used in a photo collection or a collection of various works.

In the case of gardens, they are themselves works of art. Landscape designers who are devotees to the art of gardening exist today and continue to transmit the beauty that has taken hundreds of years to perfect.

Facing my camera towards the subjects I press the shutter. Aren't they ultimately just mere reproductions? The photographs of gardens by predecessors, the statue of Buddha, the buildings... aren't they all reproductions? However, there is no mistake from the angle and position I have selected they belong to me. This is fine. This is how it is done. These photographs are the results of this selection.

Master Mirei who taught me everything is no longer with us now however, I hope you will be able to see his teachings demonstrated in my work and I look forward to your comments. In conclusion, I would like to extend my warmest gratitude to Mr. Shimpei Kusano who contributed the preface and Mr. Shigemori and designer Hiroto Kumagai for their advice. In addition, I would like to thank Mr. Akahira of Graphic-sha Publishing Co., Ltd., who was in charge of the planning and progress and especially to the former Master Mirei who I wish could have seen it. God bless you.

November, 1985

Haruzo Ohashi

大橋治三略歴

1927● 大阪市に生まれる。棚橋紫水氏に師事する
1957● 上京後フリーの写真家となる
1969●《日本の名園》(誠文堂新光社)
1973●《湖国近江》(毎日新聞社)
1976●《日本庭園史大系(全35巻)》(社会思想社)
1977●《日本庭園手法集(全5巻)》(毎日新聞社)
1980●《面打ち長沢氏春氏》(毎日新聞社)
1984●《古能面傑作集50選》(毎日新聞社)
●《修学院離宮》(新潮社)他多数
●現在、日本写真家協会・二科会会員
現住所●〒350-13 狭山市北入曽829-15 TEL.(0429)58-6567

Japanese Garden photographed by Haruzo Ohashi

四季日本の庭 大橋治三写真集

1986年1月25日●初版第1刷発行
1986年4月25日●初版第2刷発行
定　価●2,900円
著　者●大橋治三©
発行者●久世利郎
印刷所●凸版印刷株式会社
製本所●凸版印刷株式会社
写　植●株式会社 プロスタディオ
発行所●株式会社 グラフィック社
〒102 東京都千代田区九段北1-9-12
電話 03・263・4318 振替・東京3-114345
落丁・乱丁本はお取替え致します。
ISBN4-7661-0366-1 C0072 ¥2900E